THE BEST
PRE-GED
Study Series

WRITING

Lynda Rich Spiegel, M.A.
Department of English
Brandeis School, Lawrence, NY

Research & Education Association
61 Ethel Road West, Piscataway, NJ 08854

The Best PRE-GED Study Series
WRITING

Printed in the United States of America

Library of Congress Catalog Card Number 97-65280

International Standard Book Number 0-87891-801-9

Research & Education Association
61 Ethel Road West
Piscataway, New Jersey 08854

TABLE OF CONTENTS

Writing

Introduction

ABOUT THIS BOOK

This book is designed to help you strengthen the skills you will need to take the "Writing Skills" test of the **General Educational Development (GED) Examination**.

A **Pre-Test** section in the beginning of this book will help you assess the areas where you need to work the hardest. After you have completed the review areas and answered all of the drill questions, you will be given a **Post-Test** that will show your improvement in certain areas and show you which areas you still need to study. In the Post-Test section you will answer questions very similar to those you will face on the actual GED. The Pre-Test and Post-Test provide detailed explanations to all of the questions, illustrating not only why the correct answer choice was right, but also why the incorrect answer choices were wrong.

The reviews cover all areas tested on the Writing Skills test of the GED examination. Sections on the correct use of verbs, nouns, pronouns, and sentence structure, and other parts of grammar are covered extensively. Each section contains a drill so you can monitor your progress as you use this book. Entire sections are also devoted to writing an effective essay, and steps in the writing process. By mastering the skills presented in this book, you will be able to approach writing and grammar usage with confidence.

ABOUT THE GED

The GED is an examination for adults who did not complete high school and would like to earn a high school equivalency diploma. The exam is given by each state, which then issues a GED diploma. The GED is taken by adults who want or need a diploma for work,

college, or personal satisfaction. Nearly 700,000 people take the GED each year.

The GED is broken into five tests: **Writing Skills; Social Studies; Science; Interpreting Literature and the Arts; and Mathematics**. You are given about seven and a half hours to complete the examination. There are a total of 286 multiple-choice questions and an essay question on the GED examination.

There are two parts to the Writing Skills test. Part One contains 55 multiple-choice questions to be answered in 75 minutes. You will be asked to read passages and answer the questions that follow. This test is composed of 35% usage questions, and 30% spelling, punctuation, and capitalization questions. Approximately 50% of the questions on this test will deal with sentence correction, and 35% with sentence revision, while 15% of the sentence structure and usage questions will deal with construction shift. Part Two of the Writing Skills test is a 45-minute essay. Your essay must be written on the topic listed in your test booklet. You will be expected to follow all the rules for sentence structure, usage, and mechanics when writing your essay.

The GED examination is administered by the GED Testing Service of the American Council of Education (ACE) and is developed by writers who have secondary and adult education experience. Because the GED test-takers come from such diverse backgrounds, the ACE makes sure the test writers are also diverse. Once the questions have been written, they are standardized according to a certain level of difficulty and content.

The GED comes in several versions to fit the special needs of its examinees. For example, there are Spanish, French, and braille versions of the exam, as well as large-print and audio versions.

If you would like to obtain more information about the GED, such as when and where it is administered, contact your local high school or adult education center. You can also call or write to the GED Testing Service at:

1-800-62MYGED
(1-800-626-9433)
General Educational Development
GED Testing Service
American Council on Education
One Dupont Circle, NW
Washington, D.C. 20036

HOW TO USE THIS BOOK

Before you begin reading the chapters on grammar, take the Pre-Test at the front of this book. This Pre-Test will assess your current skills and indicate both your strengths and weaknesses.

This book is broken down into 14 sections, each dealing with a specific area of writing, grammar, and usage. Each section includes exercises to help you develop your skills as well as skill-building practice exercises at the end of each section to reinforce what you have learned.

It is best to move through this book chronologically because the Introduction to Grammar section lays the foundation for the rest of the book.

Because correct grammar and usage is a skill that is developed and not simply a list of facts to learn, it is important to begin developing this skill as soon as possible. Cramming for this test on the GED simply will not help. It is also wise not to try to do *too* much in one study session. There is a large amount of information presented in this book, and it will take time to digest.

When you are finished with the review sections, take the Post-Test. Compare your Post-Test score with your Pre-Test score and see how much you have improved. You may even want to take the Pre-Test again to re-evaluate your skills.

Before you begin the Pre-Test, you should take inventory of your study skills. Under what circumstances do you study best? Are you most awake in the morning, late afternoon, or evening? Do you study best under bright light, or soft? With music, or in total silence? Answer these questions and then try to optimize your study time by creating the ideal learning conditions (the atmosphere in which you learn most efficiently). Also, you should set a specific schedule for yourself that takes into consideration your other commitments. Can you study one hour each morning? A half hour every night? Two or three hours on weekends? Pick a routine and stick to it so you will be confident when it's time to take the exam.

Although you are encouraged to write in the margins of this book, you should know that you will not be allowed to mark up the texts on the actual GED examination. When you take the Post-Test, use a piece of scrap paper instead of writing in the margins of the book. This will help you be more comfortable with the actual test format.

Please note that the GED won't penalize you for guessing wrong, so if you are stuck on a question, don't leave it blank. Instead, eliminate any answers you know are not correct and choose one of the remaining options. You have a better chance of getting a question right by making an educated guess, and then you can move on to the next question. Remember, the exam is timed, so you do not want to spend too much time on any one question.

ABOUT RESEARCH AND EDUCATION ASSOCIATION

Research and Education Association (REA) is an organization of educators, scientists, and engineers who specialize in various academic fields. REA was founded in 1959 for the purpose of disseminating the most recently developed scientific information to groups in industry, government, high schools, and universities. Since then, REA has become a successful and highly respected publisher of study aids, test preps, handbooks, and reference works.

REA's publications and educational materials are highly regarded for their significant contribution to the quest for excellence that characterizes today's educational goals. We continually receive an unprecedented amount of praise from professionals, instructors, librarians, parents, and students for our books. Our authors are as diverse as the subjects and fields represented in the books we publish. They are well-known in their respective fields and serve on the faculties of prestigious universities throughout the United States.

ACKNOWLEDGMENTS

Special recognition is extended to the following persons:

Dr. M. Fogiel, President, for his overall guidance which has brought this publication to completion.

Stacey A. Sporer-Daly, Managing Editor, for directing the editorial staff throughout each phase of the project.

Kelli A. Wilkins, Project Editor, for her editorial contributions and management of the project.

Kathyrn DiGiovanni and Linda Robbian for their editorial contributions.

Marty Perzan for typesetting the manuscript.

Writing

Pre-Test

WRITING

PRE-TEST

DIRECTIONS: Read each of the sentences below and then answer the questions pertaining to them. Choose the <u>best answer choice</u> for each question.

1. The book, <u>*The Catcher in the Rye,* is read</u> by many high school students.

    (1) The book, *The Catcher In The Rye* is read . . .

    (2) The book, *the catcher in the rye* is read . . .

    (3) no error

2. <u>The milky way</u> is the name of our galaxy.

    (1) The Milky Way

    (2) The Milky way

    (3) no error

3. When you make a soufflé, you must <u>seperate</u> the eggs.

    (1) sepperate

    (2) separate

    (3) no error

4. Everyone taking the test must leave <u>their</u> backpacks outside the room.

    (1) his or her

    (2) the

    (3) no error

5. Carly feels <u>bad</u> about the entire situation.

    (1) real bad

    (2) badly

    (3) no error

6. For the past six years, I <u>worked</u> at Sears.

    (1) had worked

    (2) have been working

    (3) no error

7. <u>Between you and I,</u> she shouldn't wear so much makeup.

    (1) Between you and me

    (2) Between we two

    (3) no error

8. <u>Both Sue Ellen and myself</u> wish to welcome you.

    (1) Both Sue Ellen and me

    (2) Both Sue Ellen and I

    (3) no error

9. <u>The man that is waving</u> to you is my friend, Mitchell.

3

(1) The man who is waving

(2) The man whom is waving

(3) no error

10. Movies, which I enjoy a great deal, open weeks later in our town than they do in the city.

    (1) The movies I enjoy

    (2) The movies what I enjoy

    (3) no error

11. It was meant to be a surprise for us kids.

    (1) for we kids

    (2) for us, the kids

    (3) no error

12. Should we start shoveling now or wait for the snow to stop.

    (1) or wait for the snow to stop!

    (2) or wait for the snow to stop?

    (3) no error

13. Carlos works downtown, his wife works in the Bronx.

    (1) Carlos works downtown—his wife works in the Bronx.

    (2) Carlos works downtown; his wife works in the Bronx.

    (3) no error

14. Barkley who plays for Phoenix is one of the League's best players.

    (1) Barkley, who plays for Phoenix is one of the League's best players.

    (2) Barkley, who plays for Phoenix, is one of the League's best players.

    (3) no error

15. I have several important errands to run before we leave.

    (1) several, important

    (2) several, important,

    (3) no error

16. In any case I hope you will decide to come.

    (1) In any case I,

    (2) In any case, I

    (3) no error

17. Dear Miss Evans,

    (1) Dear Miss Evans—

    (2) Dear Miss Evans:

    (3) no error

18. Only a few men: Tony, Bill, and Jaime came to the club meeting.

    (1) Only a few men came to the club meeting: Tony, Bill, and Jaime.

    (2) Only: Tony, Bill, and Jaime came to the club meeting.

    (3) no error

19. His suit, like James, was gray.

    (1) like James'

    (2) like Jame's

    (3) no error

20. The play's ending satisfied the audience.

    (1) The plays' ending

    (2) The plays ending

    (3) no error

21. <u>Ladys</u> have gracious manners.

    (1) Ladies

    (2) Lady's

    (3) no error

22. The farmer sold all his <u>calves</u> at the auction.

    (1) calfs

    (2) calf's

    (3) no error

23. <u>There are several milks</u> now on supermarket shelves.

    (1) There are several types of milk

    (2) There are several of milk

    (3) no error

24. <u>The planning committee are</u> made up of five members.

    (1) The planning committee is

    (2) The planning committee were

    (3) no error

25. <u>They</u> have been friends for years.

    (1) Them

    (2) Their

    (3) no error

26. <u>Their both studying</u> veterinary medicine.

    (1) They're both studying

    (2) There both studying

    (3) no error

27. <u>French, Spanish Portuguese and Italian are Romance languages.</u>

    (1) French, Spanish, Portuguese and Italian are Romance languages.

    (2) French, Spanish, Portuguese, and Italian are Romance languages.

    (3) no error

28. <u>Fred skidded into a snowdrift driving down the street.</u>

    (1) Fred skidded driving down the street into a snowdrift.

    (2) Fred skidded into a snowdrift while driving down the street.

    (3) no error

29. <u>My uncle tells great stories, and jokes.</u>

    (1) My uncle tells great stories and jokes.

    (2) My uncle tells great, stories and jokes.

    (3) no error

30. <u>I enjoy great literature, classical music, and to drink fine wines.</u>

    (1) I enjoy great literature, to hear classical music, and to drink fine wines.

    (2) I enjoy great literature, classical music, and fine wines.

    (3) no error

31. <u>It was a pleasant drive the sun was shining.</u>

    (1) It was a pleasant drive because the sun was shining.

    (2) It was a pleasant drive, the sun was shining.

    (3) no error

32. That was the <u>most bravest</u> thing he ever did.

    (1) braver

    (2) bravest

    (3) no error

33. His dancing is the <u>worstest</u> I've ever seen.

    (1) worse

    (2) worst

    (3) no error

34. Carol wrapped the bandage <u>real careful.</u>

    (1) real carefully.

    (2) really carefully.

    (3) no error

35. George hid the package <u>quick-like before Barbara saw it.</u>

    (1) quick before Barbara saw it.

    (2) quickly before Barbara saw it.

    (3) no error

36. <u>As I was saying. We really should meet next week.</u>

    (1) As I was saying, we really should meet next week.

    (2) Just as I was saying, we really should meet next week.

    (3) no error

37. Yolanda <u>could of gone</u> with the others.

    (1) could have gone

    (2) would of gone

    (3) no error

38. <u>The computer and its disks have to be kept</u> in a non-humid room.

    (1) The computer and its disks has to be

    (2) The computer and its disks hast to be

    (3) no error

39. <u>For who is this phone message?</u>

    (1) Who is this phone message for?

    (2) For whom is this phone message?

    (3) no error

40. <u>Either fish or beef stew are your choice for dinner.</u>

    (1) Either fish or beef stew is your choice for dinner.

    (2) Either beef or fish stew are your choices for dinner.

    (3) no error

41. Mrs. Greenberg will be <u>dissappointed</u> if we don't come.

    (1) disappointed

    (2) dissapointed

    (3) no error

42. <u>Next week, we leave for Trinidad.</u>

    (1) Next week, we will leave for Trinidad.

    (2) Next week, we will be leaving for Trinidad.

    (3) no error

43. <u>Diana herself wrote the memo.</u>

    (1) Diana, herself, wrote the memo.

    (2) Diana herself, wrote the memo.

(3) no error

44. Dinner is served!

   (1) Dinner is served?

   (2) Dinner is served.

   (3) no error

45. Mei Ling enjoys studying English, and she finds it easy.

   (1) Mei Ling enjoys studying English because she finds it easy.

   (2) Mei Ling enjoys studying English, yet she finds it easy.

   (3) no error

46. Sam got a letter from a law firm in Lincoln Nebraska.

   (1) Lincoln, Nebraska.

   (2) Lincoln: Nebraska.

   (3) no error

47. I heard a noise downstairs; it was only the cat.

   (1) I heard a noise downstairs, it was only the cat.

   (2) I heard a noise downstairs, and it was only the cat.

   (3) no error

48. The main airport serving the Chicago vicinity is o'hare.

   (1) vicinity is O'hare.

   (2) vicinity is O'Hare.

   (3) no error

49. How many potatos should I peel for tonight's dinner?

   (1) potatoes

   (2) potatoe's

   (3) no error

50. The squirrel ran away because you walked too loud.

   (1) you walked to loud.

   (2) you walked too loudly.

   (3) no error

51. The sound of a car alarm is the annoyingst noise.

   (1) most annoyingst

   (2) most annoying

   (3) no error

52. Their will be no television until my daughter cleans her room completely.

   (1) There will be no television until my daughter cleans her room completely.

   (2) There will be no television, until my daughter cleans her room completely, I told her.

   (3) no error

53. If you have a personal problem it doesn't make sense to deal with it alone, go get some guidance.

   (1) If you have a personal problem, it doesn't make sense to deal with it alone—go get some guidance.

   (2) If you have a personal problem, it doesn't make sense to deal with it alone. Go get some guidance.

   (3) no error

54. <u>The baseball team here is as good as any other school</u>.

    (1) The baseball team here is as good as all the other schools.

    (2) The baseball team here is as good as any other school's.

    (3) no error

55. <u>I'm sure you did good on this test</u>.

    (1) I'm sure you did goodly on this test.

    (2) I'm sure you did well on this test.

    (3) no error

WRITING

ANSWER KEY

1. (3)	15. (3)	29. (1)	43. (3)
2. (1)	16. (2)	30. (2)	44. (2)
3. (2)	17. (2)	31. (1)	45. (1)
4. (1)	18. (1)	32. (2)	46. (1)
5. (3)	19. (1)	33. (2)	47. (3)
6. (2)	20. (3)	34. (2)	48. (2)
7. (1)	21. (1)	35. (2)	49. (1)
8. (2)	22. (3)	36. (1)	50. (2)
9. (1)	23. (1)	37. (1)	51. (2)
10. (3)	24. (1)	38. (3)	52. (1)
11. (3)	25. (3)	39. (2)	53. (2)
12. (2)	26. (1)	40. (1)	54. (2)
13. (2)	27. (2)	41. (1)	55. (2)
14. (2)	28. (2)	42. (1)	

PRE-TEST SELF-EVALUATION

Question Number	Subject Matter Tested	Section to Study (section, heading)
1.	Punctuation	Punctuation, commas
2.	Capitalization	Capitalization, names of astronomical bodies
2.	Nouns	Nouns, common and proper nouns
3.	Spelling	Spelling, hints for correct spelling
4.	Pronouns	Pronouns, types of pronouns
5.	Modifiers	Modifying Words, correct use of adjectives and adverbs
6.	Verbs	Verbs, tenses
7.	Pronouns	Pronouns, types of pronouns
8.	Nouns	Nouns, common and proper nouns
9.	Pronouns	Pronouns, types of pronouns
10.	Pronouns	Pronouns, types of pronouns
11.	Pronouns	Pronouns, types of pronouns
12.	Punctuation	Punctuation, end marks
13.	Sentence Structure	Sentence structure, compound sentences
14.	Nouns	Nouns, common and proper nouns
14.	Punctuation	Punctuation, commas
15.	Punctuation	Punctuation, commas
15.	Modifiers	Modifying words, adjectives
16.	Punctuation	Punctuation, commas
17.	Punctuation	Punctuation, colons and semi-colons
18.	Punctuation	Punctuation, colons and semi-colons
19.	Nouns	Nouns, possessive nouns
20.	Nouns	Nouns, possessive nouns
21.	Nouns	Nouns, forming the plural of nouns
22.	Nouns	Nouns, forming the plural of nouns
23.	Nouns	Nouns, non-countable nouns
24.	Nouns	Nouns, collective nouns
24.	Subject/Verb Agreement	Subject/verb agreement, agreement

Question Number	Subject Matter Tested	Section to Study (section, heading)
25.	Pronouns	Nouns, types of pronouns
26.	Spelling	Spelling, homonyms
27.	Punctuation	Punctuation, commas
28.	Sentence Structure	Sentence, structure, compound sentences
29.	Punctuation	Punctuation, commas
29.	Modifiers	Modifying words, adjectives
30.	Sentence Structure	Sentence structure, complex sentences
31.	Sentence Structure	Sentence structure, compound sentences
32.	Modifiers	Modifying words, correct use of adjectives and adverbs
33.	Modifiers	Modifying words, correct use of adjectives and adverbs
34.	Modifiers	Modifying words, correct use of adjectives and adverbs
35.	Modifiers	Modifying words, correct use of adjectives and adverbs
36.	Sentence Structure	Sentence structure, compound sentences
37.	Verbs	Verbs, tenses
38.	Subject/Verb Agreement	Subject/verb agreement, agreement
39.	Nouns and Pronouns	Pronouns, relative pronouns
40.	Subject/Verb Agreement	Subject/verb agreement, agreement
41.	Spelling	Spelling, hints for correct spelling
42.	Verbs	Verbs, tenses
43.	Pronouns	Pronouns, reflexive pronouns
44.	Punctuation	Punctuation, end marks
45.	Sentence Structure	Sentence structure, compound sentences
46.	Punctuation	Punctuation, commas; colons and semi-colons
47.	Sentence Structure	Sentence structure, compound sentences
48.	Capitalization	Capitalization, proper names
49.	Spelling	Spelling, hints for correct spelling
50.	Modifiers	Modifying words, correct use of adjective and adverbs

Question Number	Subject Matter Tested	Section to Study (section, heading)
51.	Modifiers	Modifying words, correct use of adjectives and adverbs
52.	Sentence Structure	Sentence structure, complex sentences
53.	Sentence Structure	Sentence structure, compound sentences
54.	Nouns	Nouns, possessive nouns
55.	Modifiers	Modifying words, correct use of adjectives and adverbs

PRE-TEST
ANSWERS AND EXPLANATIONS

1. **(3)** The most important words of titles are capitalized. (1) is incorrect because conjunctions and prepositions are not capitalized in a title.

2. **(1)** The entire name of a proper noun is capitalized, not merely the first word.

3. **(2)** Both the original sentence and (1) misspell the word.

4. **(1)** The word "everyone" is a singular indefinite pronoun. In order for all parts of the sentence to agree, the possessive pronoun must also be singular. (2) is incorrect because the sentence calls for a possessive pronoun; the backpacks must belong to someone.

5. **(3)** (1) is incorrect because "real" is an adjective, not an adverb. The adjective "bad" requires an adverb, "really," to describe the intensity of Carly's emotion. (2) is incorrect because the verb "feels" in this sentence is a linking verb. A linking verb requires a predicate adjective to describe how Carly feels. The word "badly" is an adverb.

6. **(2)** The correct answer uses the present perfect progressive tense. This tense is used when an action was begun in the past and is currently still in progress. (1) is incorrect because the past perfect tense implies that the person no longer works at Sears.

7. **(1)** The word "between" is a preposition. Prepositions are always accompanied by their objects. The pronoun "me" is an object. (2) is incorrect because the pronoun "we" is a subject.

8. **(2)** The original sentence incorrectly uses the reflexive pronoun. (1) is incorrect because Sue Ellen and the unnamed person are the compound subjects of the sentence, and "me" is an object pronoun. The correct answer uses a subject pronoun.

9. **(1)** The original sentence uses the relative pronoun "that" in referring to a person when it should only be used for specific things. The correct relative pronoun should be a subject pronoun, since it refers to the man who is the subject of the sentence. (2) is incorrect since "whom" is an object pronoun.

10. **(3)** The relative pronoun "which" refers to things in general. (1) is incorrect because it is missing a relative pronoun, and (2) is incorrect because it doesn't make sense.

11. **(3)** The word "for" is a preposition and always requires an object. (1) is incorrect because it uses a subject pronoun instead of an object pronoun. (2) is incorrect because the tag line, "the kids," is unnecessary.

12. **(2)** Since the original sentence asks a question, it must have a question mark as an end mark.

13. **(2)** The original sentence is a run-on since it consists of two complete sentences on each side of the comma. (1) is incorrect because a dash is never used to separate two parts of a sentence.

14. **(2)** The phrase, "who plays for Phoenix," modifies the subject of the sentence, Barkley. Whenever a modifying word or phrase is used to interrupt a sentence, it should be offset by commas.

15. **(3)** A sentence with more than one adjective or adverb usually separates these words with a comma. However, when the words *must* appear in a specific order to make sense, commas are not used.

16. **(2)** Introductory phrases such as "In any case" are always set off by a comma. (1) is incorrect because the comma was placed after the subject instead of after the introductory phrase.

17. **(2)** In a business letter a colon is always used after the name of the person being addressed.

18. **(1)** Colons are used before a list; however, they must be preceded by a complete sentence, as in (1).

19. **(1)** When a noun ends in "s," the correct way to show possession is to place the apostrophe after the final "s." The original sentence neglected to include an apostrophe; (2) incorrectly placed the apostrophe.

20. **(3)** In the original sentence, the noun "play" is singular and needs only an apostrophe and "s" to make it possessive. (1) is incorrect because it turns the singular noun into a plural noun. (2) is incorrect because it is missing an apostrophe.

21. **(1)** The correct way to make singular nouns which end in a "y" preceded by a consonant plural is to change the "y" to "i" and add "es."

22. **(3)** The correct way to make most one-syllable singular nouns which end in "f" plural is to change the "f" to "ves."

23. **(1)** "Milk" is a collective noun; it cannot be counted. In order to count "several" milks, the word must be placed into a countable unit of measurement. Using the words "types of milk" is correct since it places something uncountable into a countable unit.

24. **(1)** "Committee" is a collective noun. All collective nouns are singular. The original sentence uses a plural form of the verb (are). (1) uses the singular verb (is), thereby creating subject and verb agreement in the sentence.

25. **(3)** The pronoun "they" is a subject pronoun; it was used correctly in the original sentence since "they" is the subject of the sentence. (1) is incorrect because "them" is an object pronoun. (2) is incorrect because "their" is a possessive pronoun.

26. **(1)** "Their," "they're," and "there" are homophones. Even though they sound alike, they have different meanings. "Their" is a possessive pronoun; "there" is an adverb showing where something took place; and "they're" is a contraction of the words "they are."

27. **(2)** All items on a list are separated by a comma unless they are meant to be considered as one.

28. **(2)** The original sentence contains a misplaced modifier, "driving down the street." The sentence reads as if the snowdrift was doing the driving, instead of Fred. It needs a word such as "while" to avoid this comic misunderstanding.

29. **(1)** The sentence does not need any commas since "stories and jokes" are compound objects of the verb "tells." The original sentence is incorrect since two items do not constitute a list; therefore, there is no need for a comma. (2) is incorrect because a comma never separates an adjective from the noun it is next to.

30. **(2)** Both the original sentence and (1)

lack parallel structure. Only in (2) are all the components of the sentence written in the same form.

31. **(1)** Both the original sentence and (2) are run-on sentences. The original lacks punctuation and (2) uses a comma incorrectly.

32. **(2)** When using adjectives to compare, never combine "-est" with the words "most" or "least." (1) is incorrect because it uses the comparative form of the adjective instead of the superlative form.

33. **(2)** The adjective "bad" is irregular. When used in the superlative form, it is "worst." (1) is incorrect because it is the comparative form of the adjective in a sentence where the superlative is needed.

34. **(2)** The verb "wrapped" is modified by the adverb "carefully." The original sentence incorrectly used the adjective "careful." (1) is incorrect because the word "real," which modifies the adverb "carefully," is an adjective. Only an adverb can modify an adjective, another adjective cannot. Only (2) uses both words in their correct adverb formats.

35. **(2)** There is no such word as "quicklike." (1) is incorrect because the verb "hid" needs an adverb to modify it, and "quick" is an adjective.

36. **(1)** Both the original sentence and (2) are sentence fragments. Neither of them contain a complete thought. (1) completes the thought by providing a main clause.

37. **(1)** The conditional words, "could," "should," and "would" are never followed by the preposition "of," but rather by the verb "have."

38. **(3)** When one part of a compound sub-

ject is plural and the other part is singular, the verb must agree with the part that is nearest to it. Since the word "disks" is plural and is nearer to the plural verb "have," the original sentence is correct. (1) is incorrect because the verb "has" is singular. (2) is incorrect because "hast" is an archaic form of the words "has to."

39. **(2)** The original sentence is incorrect because the preposition "for" needs to be followed by an object; "who" is a subject. (1) is technically incorrect even though it is acceptable in common spoken usage. (2) is correct because "for" is followed by an object, "whom."

40. **(1)** The conjunctions "either . . . or" divide the two things under consideration into singular units. Since both fish and beef stew are to be considered as singular, the verb must also be singular. Both the original sentence and (2) use the plural verb "are," instead of the singular verb "is." Switching the order of the words as in (2) does not affect the subject and verb agreement.

41. **(1)** Both the original sentence and (2) misspell the word "disappointed."

42. **(1)** The phrase "next week" tells us the action of leaving will be performed in the future. (2) is incorrect because it uses the future progressive tense of the verb, which implies that we will be in the process of leaving when something else will happen, although the sentence does not offer any information to that effect. It merely states that an action will take place in the future. Therefore, (1), which uses the future simple tense, is correct.

43. **(3)** Reflexive pronouns are not set off by commas.

44. **(2)** "Dinner is served" is a simple sentence. The original incorrectly uses an excla-

mation mark, which is used to indicate excitement. If overused, it loses its impact. (1) is incorrect since it is a question, not a statement.

45. **(1)** Both the original sentence and (2) join the two complete sentences using illogical conjunctions. (1) is correct because the conjunction "because" shows a logical cause and effect between the two parts of the sentence.

46. **(1)** A comma always separates the name of a city or town from its state.

47. **(3)** (1) is a run-on sentence. (2) uses an illogical conjunction, "and," to join the two parts of the sentence. The original correctly uses a semicolon to join two related complete sentences into one.

48. **(2)** The first letter in proper nouns is capitalized. Since "O'Hare" is a contraction of two old Irish names, both the "O" and the "H" need to be capitalized.

49. **(1)** Both the original sentence and (2) misspell the plural form of the noun "potato."

50. **(2)** The verb "walked" must be described by an adverb. The original sentence uses an adjective, "loud," instead of the adjec-tive "loudly." (1) is incorrect because it uses the preposition "to" instead of the adverb "too."

51. **(2)** When forming the superlative form of an adjective, never combine "-est" with the words "most" or "least."

52. **(1)** The original sentence uses the wrong form of "their," and (2) uses unnecessary commas.

53. **(2)** Both the original and (1) are run-on sentences. They both contain too much information for one sentence. In (2), the ideas have been correctly punctuated.

54. **(2)** A comparison is being made between the teams at the school "here" and the teams at other schools. Another way to write "the teams at other schools" is to use the possessive, "other school's teams." (2) is correct because it is the only sentence which uses the possessive. The word "teams" is understood and need not be written.

55. **(2)** The verb "did" needs an adverb to describe it. The original sentence is incorrect because the word "good" is an adjective. (1) is incorrect because the adverb form of "good" is "well."

Introduction to Grammar

WRITING

INTRODUCTION TO GRAMMAR

THE SENTENCE AND ITS PARTS

A **sentence** is a group of words that makes sense, ending with a period, exclamation point, or question mark. It is the most basic unit of written communication. Every sentence, unless it is a command, has at least a subject and a verb.

<u>Elephants</u> never <u>forget.</u>
  subject   verb

<u>Life</u> <u>is</u> sweet.
subject verb

When a sentence is a command, the subject is usually unspoken, but is understood to be the person being addressed.

<u>Bring</u> four units of O negative blood to
verb

Emergency!

<u>Get</u> out!
verb

Subjects

The **subject** is the topic of the sentence. It states what the sentence is about. The subject is usually a noun or pronoun. To find the subject, ask yourself who or what is the topic of the sentence.

Miss Fumiko graded the essays.

Who graded the essays? *Miss Fumiko* did. The subject of the sentence is *Miss Fumiko*.

Verbs

The **verb** expresses action or a state of being. These terms will be further explained in greater detail in the chapters devoted to verb tenses and to subject and verb agreement.

Objects

When a verb shows action, the subject is the person or thing who does the action. The word that receives the action is called an **object**. In the sentences below, the objects have been underlined for you.

Su Yuan studied <u>physics</u>.

Gil invited <u>Darren</u> and <u>Adam</u>.

My camera takes great <u>pictures</u>.

Give <u>me</u> a <u>break</u>!

The way to find the object of a sentence is to first locate the subject and the verb.

Su Yuan studied physics.

Su Yuan is the subject because she is the topic of the sentence. The verb is *studied* because that is what is being done; Su Yuan is studying something. Next, ask yourself who or what is being studied. The answer is *physics*. Therefore, *physics* is the object of the verb.

Gil invited Darren and Adam.

Gil is the subject, again, because he is the topic of the sentence. The verb is *invited* because that is what is being done. Ask yourself who or what is being invited. The answer is *Darren* and *Adam*. Therefore, they are the compound object of the verb.

> My camera takes great pictures.

Since the topic of the sentence is the camera, *camera* is the subject of the sentence. *Takes* is the verb; that is what cameras do. Ask yourself what in this sentence is being taken. The answer is *pictures*. Therefore, *pictures* is the object of the sentence.

> Give me a break!

Since this sentence is a command, the subject is understood to be the person being spoken to. *Give* is the verb. Ask yourself what in this sentence is being given. The answer is *a break*. Therefore, *break* is the object of the verb *give*. When a verb has an object, it is called the direct object. Sometimes, a sentence with a direct object also has an indirect object. To find out if a sentence has an indirect object, look for a noun or pronoun that tells to whom or for whom the action was done. In this sentence, the *break* was given to *me*. Therefore, *me* is the indirect object. One clue is that indirect objects always appear before the direct object, never after.

Linking Verbs

When a verb shows a state of being, it is called a **linking verb** since it links the subject to a word that describes it. These describing words can be either nouns, pronouns, or adjectives. When used with linking verbs, they are called predicate nouns or pronouns, or predicate adjectives.

Any form or tense of the verb *to be* is considered a linking verb: am, is, are, was, or were. Some verbs that are usually considered action verbs [taste, feel, sound, grow, or smell] are linking verbs in certain sentences. In the following sentences, the linking verbs have been underlined.

> I <u>am</u> a writer.

The subject *I* is linked to the predicate noun *writer*.

> Richard and Judy <u>are</u> my cousins.

The subjects *Richard* and *Judy* are linked to the predicate noun *cousins*.

> Your suit <u>is</u> very stylish.

The subject *suit* is linked to the predicate adjective *stylish*.

> Mother Theresa <u>is</u> unselfish.

The subject *Mother Theresa* is linked to the predicate adjective *unselfish*.

> Dinner <u>smells</u> delicious.

The subject *dinner* is linked to the predicate adjective *delicious*. If you are confused because *smells* appears to be an action verb, ask yourself if any action is being performed by the subject of the sentence. Is the dinner smelling anything? Of course not. The word *smells* in this sentence shows a state of being, or a condition of the dinner. It smells delicious. If you substituted the verb *tastes* in this sentence, it would also be a linking verb for the same reason.

> Sam <u>feels</u> angry.

The subject *Sam* is linked to the predicate adjective *angry*. In this sentence, *feels* is a linking verb because there is no action; Sam isn't physically touching anything. He is experiencing an emotion. As a test, see if you can substitute a form of the verb *to be* for the verb in question. If you can, the verb is a linking verb. In this case, you could say *Sam is angry*. Therefore, *feels* is a linking verb in this sentence.

> Claudia <u>grew</u> hysterical.

The subject *Claudia* is linked to the predicate adjective *hysterical*. There is no action; Claudia isn't growing vegetables, she is experiencing an emotional condition. Try the substitution test. It is possible to say *Claudia is hysterical* without changing the meaning of the sentence.

Questions

For the following, locate the subject in each sentence.

1. The most popular television show in my house is "ER."

2. We work at the post office.

3. Into the night rode Paul Revere.

4. Sacramento is the capital of California.

5. From far away came the marching army.

For each sentence with an action verb, circle the objects. Write DO for each direct object and IO for each indirect object.

```
            IO        DO
ex:  Angela sold him a used computer.
```

Some of the sentences contain linking verbs. For each sentence with a linking verb, circle the predicate noun or predicate adjective. Write PN for each predicate noun and PA for each predicate adjective.

```
              PN
ex:  Boston is an exciting city.
```

6. The company gave me a season ticket.

7. Mr. Nelson is a gentleman.

8. Danielle is my student.

9. Deena baked some brownies.

10. Many African-Americans celebrate Kwanza.

11. Connie looks pleased.

12. Thai food is hot.

13. Starks made a three-point basket.

14. The children drew us a picture.

15. Give Alice some help.

Answers

1. *"ER"* is the subject.

2. *We* is the subject.

3. *Paul Revere* is the subject

4. *Sacramento* is the subject.

5. *army* is the subject.

6. *ticket* is the object.

7. *gentleman* is a predicate noun.

8. *student* is a predicate noun.

9. *brownies* is the object.

10. *Kwanza* is the object.

11. *pleased* is the predicate adjective.

12. *hot* is the predicate adjective.

13. *basket* is the object.

14. *picture* is the direct object; *us* is the indirect object.

15. *help* is the direct object; *Alice* is the indirect object.

OTHER PARTS OF THE SENTENCE

Many sentences are made up of more than just the subject, verb, and its object or predicate word.

Conjunctions

Conjunctions are words which join together different parts of the sentence. The most common conjunctions are "and," "or," "but," "either...or," and "neither...nor." Conjunctions will be discussed in greater detail in the section on commas. The main thing to know about conjunctions is that their function is to connect one part of a sentence to another.

Adjectives and Adverbs

Adjectives and **adverbs** are known as modifiers since they change words by providing more detail about the words they describe. They are invaluable parts of the sentence since they help make the writer's ideas vivid and easily recognizable. For more information about the way adjectives and adverbs function in a sentence, see Modifying Words.

Prepositions and Prepositional Phrases

Prepositions and **prepositional phrases** are used to indicate a thing's location or function. Like adjectives and adverbs, they are details which enhance the reader's understanding of the subject. Like conjunctions, prepositions are connecting words; they connect the word or words that follow them (called the object of the prepositions) with some other part of the sentence.

The following is a list of frequently used prepositions:

at	by
for	down
on	through
about	around
under	behind
with	into
over	across
beside	in
toward	of
among	between

In the following sentences, the prepositions have been underlined:

They went <u>into</u> the house. (shows the location — where they went)

We spent New Year's Eve <u>with</u> our friends. (shows location — where we spent New Year's Eve)

<u>Over</u> the river and <u>through</u> the woods, <u>to</u> Grandmother's house we go. (all these prepositions show location — they give directions to Grandmother's house)

Walk <u>around</u> the side <u>of</u> the house and put the groceries <u>on</u> the deck. (shows location — how to get to the deck and where to put the groceries)

Have a glass <u>of</u> wine <u>with</u> dinner. (shows function — the glass contains wine; shows location — the wine will be had with dinner)

List the prepositions in the following paragraph.

Question

Between New York and Chicago, we came upon two strange signs that kept us inside the car. For hours, we stayed on the road contrary to our plan, with those signs reappearing before our eyes long after they had disappeared from our sight.

Answer

Between; upon; inside; for; on; to; with; before; after; from

LABELING THE SENTENCE

Learning to label all the parts of a sentence can really help you gain a better understanding of how the English language is structured. Once you have the rationale firmly in your mind, you will discover that you are making fewer mistakes when you write. In the following sentences, we have gone into great detail to help you label all the parts of the sentence and, more importantly, to understand the methods you can use to check your answers.

Questions

Mr. Sakura made us dinner.

1. What is the topic of the sentence? Who is it about?

2. What action has Mr. Sakura performed?

3. What did Mr. Sakura make?

4. For whom did Mr. Sakura make dinner?

Sol and Eileen traveled to Florida.

5. What is the topic of the sentence? Who is it about?

6. What action have Sol and Eileen performed?

7. Where have Sol and Eileen traveled?

We are a large, happy family.

8. What is the topic of the sentence? Who is the sentence about?

9. What action have *we* performed?

10. What word does the linking verb link the subject to?

11. What do the words *large* and *happy* tell you about the family?

Hector waited patiently.

12. What is the topic of the sentence? Who is the sentence about?

13. What action is being performed by Hector?

14. In what manner is Hector waiting? In other words, how is he waiting?

Morty is a very good-looking man.

15. What is the topic of the sentence? Who is the sentence about?

16. What action is Morty performing?

17. What type of man is Morty?

18. To what extent is Morty good-looking?

Answers

1. The sentence is about Mr. Sakura. Therefore, *Mr. Sakura* is the subject of the sentence.

2. Mr. Sakura has *made* something. *Made* is an action; therefore, *made* is an action verb.

3. Mr. Sakura made dinner. Since *dinner* answers the question, "what did Mr. Sakura make?" it is the direct object of the verb.

4. Mr. Sakura made dinner for us. If a sentence has a direct object, it might also have an indirect object. Since the question "For whom was the dinner made?" can be answered, the answer *us* is the indirect object.

5. This sentence is concerned with two people, Sol and Eileen. Therefore, the sentence has a compound subject, *Sol and Eileen*.

6. They have traveled. Since *travel* is an action, the action verb in this sentence is *traveled*.

7. They have traveled to Florida. The phrase *to Florida* gives the location of their travel. *To Florida* is a prepositional phrase giving more detail about the destination of Sol and Eileen's trip.

8. The sentence is about an unnamed group of people. The word *we* is a pronoun taking the place of the names of all the people in the family. Since the sentence is about all these people — whoever they are — the subject of the sentence is *we*.

9. There is no action in this sentence. The word *are* is a form of the verb *to be*. *Are* is a linking verb.

10. It links the subject *we* to the predicate noun *family*. It is the same as saying, *we = family*.

11. Both *large* and *happy* describe the family. They tell you what kind of family it is. Therefore, *large* and *happy* are adjectives, since they modify the noun *family*.

12. The sentence is about Hector. He is the subject of the sentence.

13. Hector is waiting. *Waiting* is the action verb.

14. Hector is waiting patiently. Since the word *patiently* gives us details about how Hector waits, the word *patiently* is an adverb modifying the verb *waiting*.

15. The sentence is about Morty. He is the subject of the sentence.

16. There is no action in this sentence. The word *is* is a linking verb, joining the subject *Morty* to the predicate noun *man*. It is the same as saying *Morty = man*.

17. Morty is a good-looking man. The word *good-looking* is an adjective, giving more detail about the noun *man*.

18. Morty is very good-looking. Since the word *very* tells us to what extent Morty is good-looking, it is an adverb modifying the adjective *good-looking*.

		action			object of the preposition
---	subject	verb	adverb	preposition	
					↓
example:	Lauren	ran	frantically	[to the day care center.]
				prepositional phrase	

☞ Practice: Labeling Sentences

DIRECTIONS: Write the part of speech of each word in the below sentences. See the example above.

1. All men are created equal.

2. Mary had a little lamb.

3. Here we go around the mulberry bush.

4. *Sports Illustrated* is a widely read magazine.

5. Robbie is looking for a job.

6. Jack walked to the video store.

7. Many children take piano lessons.

8. There are ten students in the class.

9. Lynn works at the bank.

10. *USA Today* is a popular newspaper.

Answers

1. *All* — adjective telling how many, *men* — subject, *are created* — linking verb, *equal* — predicate adjective

2. *Mary* — subject, *had* — action verb, *little* — adjective, *lamb* — direct object

3. *Here* — adverb, *we* — subject, *go* — action verb, *around* — preposition, *the mulberry bush* — object of the preposition

4. *Sports Illustrated* — subject, *is* — linking verb, *widely* — adverb, *read* — adjective, *magazine* — predicate noun

5. *Robbie* — subject, *is looking* — action verb, *for* — preposition, *job* — object of the preposition

6. *Jack* — subject, *walked* — action verb, *to* — object of the preposition, *store* — object of the preposition

7. *Many* — adjective telling how many, *children* — subject, *take* — action verb, *piano* — adjective, *lessons* — direct object

8. *There* — adverb, *are* — linking verb, *ten* — adjective, *students* — subject, *in* — preposition, *class* — object of the preposition

9. *Lynn* — subject, *works* — action verb, *at* — preposition, *bank* — object of the preposition

10. *USA Today* — subject, *is* — linking verb, *popular* — adjective, *newspaper* — noun

REVIEW

Many people find the study of grammar intimidating. There seem to be so many rules to follow, and for many people, the memorization of these rules is the entire point of studying grammar. Actually, nothing could be further from the truth. While it is important to be *aware* of grammatical rules, there is little point in memorizing them. Most often, a question can be resolved by consulting a grammar rule book, such as REA's *Handbook of English: Grammar, Style, and Writing*. Rather than encouraging students to sit down every night after a long day of work and memorize the rules of English grammar, this section has been written with the intention of making readers comfortable with the logic behind the language. We have described the main parts of speech so that you will become familiar with grammatical terms and how they function in writing. Readers will discover that they can begin to recognize parts of speech when reading the newspaper and listening to the television. They may even start to discover errors in memos or other forms of writing that you see at work! So, instead of approaching this book with trepidation, relax and be confident that grammar won't "own" you; it is simply a tool to enhance understanding of the language.

Remember, a basic sentence in the English language contains at least a subject and a verb. Sometimes, when issuing an order, the subject of the sentence is understood to be "you," the person being addressed. Some verbs express action; these verbs often are followed by "objects," which receive the action. Some action verbs have no objects, while linking verbs never have objects since they express a state of being, not an action. Other parts of the

sentence exist to embellish the basic meaning. Conjunctions join shorter sentences in order to create a longer, logically connected sentence. Prepositions, like conjunctions, connect parts of the sentence. They also indicate a noun's location or function. Adjectives and adverbs make sentences lively by providing descriptive detail.

Some of the exercises in this section ask you to label parts of the sentence. Doing so will give you a clear picture of how the various parts of speech function together. Once you are able to do these exercises perfectly, try labeling some of the sentences you see in the newspaper, or in the novel you are reading. Do you notice how different writers vary their sentence structures? This variation in sentencing is the writer's individual style. Before long, you will have developed your own personal style of writing. This book will help you make sure that *your* style is a correct one. Good luck!

Writing

Verbs

WRITING

VERBS

ACTION AND LINKING VERBS

Every sentence must have a verb. Verbs express action or a state of being. The term "state of being" is used to describe what a person, place, or thing is or is like. When a verb shows action it is called an **action verb**. When it expresses a state of being it is called a **linking verb** because it links the subject of the sentence to a word which describes it.

The following is a list of linking verbs and action verbs:

Verb Lists

Linking Verbs	Action Verbs
am, are, is, was, were (all forms of "to be")	to dance
	to play
	to run
taste	to love
feel	to fix
smell	to jump
grow	to have
seem	to hold

taste, feel, smell, grow, seem: These words can be linking verbs, depending on how they are used in a sentence.

The list of action verbs is endless, but it includes all the linking verbs mentioned above, with the exception of "to be." The verbs in the sentences are underlined.

Elliot <u>dances</u> every weekend.
(shows action)

Danielle <u>is</u> a good student.
(shows state of being)

Morgan <u>plays</u> the piano.
(shows action)

Joshua <u>seems</u> sad.
(shows state of being)

Your cologne <u>smells</u> wonderful.
(shows state of being)

Weng <u>plays</u> guitar.
(shows action)

You need to be aware of whether a verb is an action verb or a linking verb. Sentences with action verbs frequently have an object which "receives" the action. Sentences with linking verbs are completed with either a predicate noun, a predicate pronoun, or a predicate adjective which describes the subject. Remember, these predicate words "link" the subject of the sentence to a word which describes it.

SUBJECT / VERB AGREEMENT

A verb can be either singular or plural. The terms singular or plural refer to the form of the verb which matches the subject. If the subject is a singular noun, then the verb must also be written in its singular form. If the subject is a plural noun, the verb must also be written in its plural form. In the sentences below, notice how the verb is either singular or plural, depending on the subject of the sentence.

I <u>am</u> happy to be here.
(singular — *I* is a singular subject)

Joe and Angel <u>are</u> not so sure of the date.
(plural — *Joe* and *Angel* are plural subjects)

Gerald <u>loves</u> chocolate cake.

(singular — *Gerald* is a singular subject)

Sandie and Peter <u>love</u> to go sailing.
(plural — *Sandie* and *Peter* are plural subjects)

The baby <u>has</u> a cold.
(singular — *baby* is a singular subject)

They <u>have</u> a house in the country.
(plural — *they* is a plural subject)

A verb must agree with the subject of the sentence. See the section on subject and verb agreement on page 39 for a more detailed explanation.

[I, you, we, they] <u>hope</u> you will stay.

[He, she] <u>hopes</u> you will stay.

[I, you, we, they] grow.

[He, she, it, one] grows.

TENSES

Tense means time. Verbs have the ability to tell us not only what action is occurring, but also when it is occurring. The form of a verb changes in order to indicate when an action takes place. The chart shown below demonstrates the important verb tenses in English.

The **simple tenses** of the verb are just as it sounds: they are simply the verb without any additional words. The **progressive tenses** refer to an action in progress, whether it is currently in progress, was in progress at a certain time in the past, or will be in progress at a certain time in the future. Progressive tenses are always written with a helping verb, some form of the verb "to be." The **perfect tenses** are always written with a helping verb, some form of the verb "to have." They are a bit more complicated and are explained in detail below.

The **present perfect tense** is used for an action that began in the past but continues into the future.

I <u>have</u> <u>lived</u> in Indianapolis all my life.

The **past perfect tense** is used for an action that occurred earlier, but is mentioned now.

Mrs. Tran ate the apple that she <u>had</u> <u>picked</u> earlier.
(first she picked it, then she ate it)

The **future perfect tense** is used for an action that will have been completed at a specific time in the future.

In September, I <u>will</u> <u>have</u> <u>given</u> birth.
(September is the specific time in the future. At that time, the action of giving birth will have been completed.)

In the following sentences, notice the rationale for the use of each verb tense.

	Simple	Progressive	Perfect
Past	action is completed	action was in progress until interruption	action completed before another action
Present	action occurs on a regular basis, or is ongoing	action is ongoing right now	action began in past, but is completed in present
Future	action expected to happen	action will be in progress at some future time	action will be completed prior to another action

Last week, I <u>saw</u> that movie.
>(past simple — the action occurred in the past)

Mothers <u>love</u> their children.
>(present simple — this action regularly occurs on an on-going basis)

I <u>will</u> <u>leave</u> tomorrow.
>(future simple — the action will occur in the future)

They <u>were</u> <u>looking</u> for her when she called.
>(past progressive — at some point in the past, an action was in progress when something interrupted it)

I <u>am</u> <u>studying</u> right now.
>(present progressive — the action is occurring at the present)

I <u>have</u> <u>been</u> <u>waiting</u> for a long time now.
>(present perfect progressive — the action began in the past — a long time ago — and is currently still in progress)

We <u>had</u> <u>been</u> <u>looking</u> for a new couch when we finally found the right one.
>(past perfect progressive — the action was in progress at some point in the past when it was completed because another action interrupted it — they found the right one)

By midnight, she <u>will</u> <u>have</u> <u>been</u> <u>studying</u> for three hours.
>(future perfect progressive — at some point in the future the action that was in progress will have been completed)

As you can see, tenses are formed by combining the three basic tenses: past, present, and future, with the basic forms of simple, progressive, and perfect.

COMMON ERRORS

It is not necessary to learn the names of all these tenses; they are mentioned only so that you can gain a better understanding of the logic behind the language. The most important thing to learn is to avoid common errors by using the correct forms.

The following examples demonstrate the most commonly made errors in verb tense.

Yesterday, I <u>says</u> to my sister, "Come over on Friday."

Since the action took place in the past (yesterday), the verb must be written in the past tense. Since "says" is the present tense, it is incorrect. Therefore, the sentence should be written as follows:

Yesterday, I <u>said</u> to my sister, "Come over on Friday."

Next week, I <u>begin</u> study for the GED.

Since the action will not take place until some time in the future (next week), the verb must be written in the future tense. Since "begin" is the present tense, it is incorrect. The sentence should read as follows:

Next week, I <u>will</u> <u>begin</u> studying for the GED.

The dog <u>attacked</u> the cat after she <u>scratched</u> him.

The dog did not attack the cat until the cat first attacked him. Thus, the action of scratching was completed before the attacking took place. In order to show this sequence correctly, use the past perfect tense. The sentence should read as follows:

The dog <u>attacked</u> the cat after she <u>had</u> <u>scratched</u> him.

A commonly overheard error with verb tenses involves confusing the present progressive with the present simple. Very often, people use the progressive tense incorrectly. This mistake is very easy to avoid if you understand exactly when to use either tense. Use the present progressive tense ONLY if you are describing an action that is currently in progress at that moment.

For example, you could say, "Right now, I <u>am</u> <u>studying</u> for the GED exam." The present simple tense is used to refer to things that are generally true at any given time. For instance, it is correct to say, "Mrs. Kastin <u>caters</u> parties," if this is something she does on a regular basis. In response to the question, "What does Mrs. Kastin do?" the answer should use the present simple tense, since people do what they do on a regular basis. Therefore, it is always incorrect to answer a question such as, "What do you do?" or "Where do you live?" by using the progressive tense.

☞ Practice: Verbs

> **DIRECTIONS:** Fill in the blank with the requested form of the verb in parentheses.

1. I _____ next year. (to graduate, future simple)

2. Right now, I _____ for the pre-GED exam. (to study, present progressive)

3. I _____ for the past three hours. (to shop, present perfect progressive)

4. Before dinner, I _____ all the laundry. (to fold, past perfect)

5. Any day now, she _____ about the new job. (to hear, future simple)

6. The sun _____ in the east. (to rise, present simple)

7. Yesterday, the sun _____ at 6 a.m. (to rise, past simple)

8. As of June, I _____ for six years. (to study, future perfect progressive)

9. We _____ when our friends came to visit. (to read, past progressive)

10. I _____ when the alarm rang. (to awake, past simple)

11. I _____ 50 pages by tomorrow. (to read, future simple)

12. We _____ in the church choir. (to sing, past simple)

13. He _____ class on Mondays and Wednesdays. (to teach, present simple)

14. You _____ my sweater without permission. (to take, past simple)

15. It _____ once spring arrives. (to grow, future simple)

16. The bee _____ her while she was weeding the garden. (to sting, past simple)

17. He _____ many Broadway plays. (to cast, past perfect)

18. He _____ the plane tomorrow if the skies are clear. (to fly, future progressive)

19. They _____ furniture all afternoon. (to choose, present perfect progressive)

20. You should _____ your ticket before the train arrived. (to buy, past perfect progressive)

Answers

1. *will graduate* — future simple. **Will** is a helping verb that points to the future. **Graduate** is the simple form of the verb "to graduate." The word **next** signals the future. **Will graduate** shows the action (**graduate**) will occur in the future. According to the sentence, the subject **I** will graduate at a future time (**next year**).

2. *am studying* — present progressive. The helping verb **am** is a form of "to be." A form of the verb "to be" is needed for the progressive tense. **Am studying** shows the action (**studying**) is occurring at the present (**right now**). According to the sentence, the subject **I** is in the process of studying for the pre-GED exam at the present time (**right now**).

3. *have been shopping* — present perfect progressive. The helping verb **have** is a form of "to have." A form of the verb "to have" is needed for the perfect tense. The helping verb **been** is a form of "to be." A form of the verb "to be" is needed for the progressive tense. **Have been shopping** shows the action (**shopping**) began in the past (**three hours**) and is still in progress. According to the sentence, the subject **I** began shopping three hours ago and is continuing to shop at the present time.

4. *had folded* — past perfect. The helping verb **had** is the past tense form of "to have." A form of the verb "to have" is needed for the perfect tense. **Had folded** shows the action (**folded the laundry**) occurred earlier (**before dinner**) but is mentioned now. According to the sentence, the subject **I** had folded the laundry; then ate dinner.

5. *will hear* — future simple. **Will** is a helping verb that points to the future. **Hear** is the simple form of the verb "to hear." **Will hear** shows the action (**hear**) will occur in the future (**any day**). According to the sentence, the subject **she** will hear about her new job in the future (**any day**).

6. *rises* — present simple. The verb **rises** shows an action occurs on a regular on-going basis. The subject of the sentence is **sun**. The pronoun substitute for **sun** is **it**. The present simple form of the verb "to rise" should end in **-s**. According to the sentence, the subject **sun** rises on a regular on-going basis in the east.

7. *rose* — past simple. The verb shows the action occurred in the past. **Rose** is the simple past form of the verb "to rise." The word **yesterday** signals the previous day (the past). According to the sentence, the subject **sun** rose at 6 a.m. the previous day (**yesterday**).

8. *will have been studying* — future perfect progressive. **Will** is a helping verb that points to the future. The helping verb **have** is a form of "to have." A form of the verb "to have" is needed for the perfect tense. **Been** is a form of "to be." A form of "to be" is needed for the progressive tense. **Will have been studying** shows that at some point in the future (**six years**) the action (**studying**) will have been completed (**as of June**). According to the sentence, the subject **I** will have been studying for six years as of June.

9. *were reading* — past progressive. The helping verb **were** is the past tense form of the verb "to be." The past tense form of the verb "to be" is needed for the past progressive tense. **Were reading** shows the action (**reading**) was in progress in the past when something (**friends came to visit**) interrupted it. According to the sentence, the subject **we** was in the process of reading when the arrival of the friends interrupted the reading.

10. *awoke* — past simple. The verb **awoke** shows the action occurred in the past. **Awoke** is the past tense form of the verb "to awake." According to the sentence, the subject **I** awoke when the alarm rang.

11. *will read* — future simple. **Will** is a helping verb that points to the future. **Read** is the simple form of the verb "to read." The word **tomorrow** signals the future. **Will read** shows the action (**read**) will occur in the future (**tomorrow**). According to the sentence, the subject **I** will read 50 pages by some point in the future (**tomorrow**).

12. *sang* — past simple. The verb **sang** shows the action occurred in the past. **Sang** is the past tense form of "to sing."

13. *teaches* — present simple. **Teaches** is the present simple form of "to teach." **Teaches** shows the action occurs on an on-going basis. The subject of the sentence is **he**. **He** is the pronoun substitute for a man's name. The present simple form of the verb should end in **-s**. According to the sentence, the subject **he** teaches the class on a regular on-going basis (**Mondays and Wednesdays**).

14. *took* — past simple. **Took** shows the action is completed. **Took** is the simple past form of "to take."

15. *will grow* — future simple. **Will** is a help-ing verb that points to the future. **Grow** is the simple form of the verb "to grow." **Will grow** shows that the action (**grow**) will occur in the future (**once spring arrives**). According to the sentence, the subject **it** will grow in the future (**when spring arrives**).

16. *stung* — past simple. **Stung** shows the action occurred in the past. **Stung** is the simple past form of the verb "to sting."

17. *had cast* — past perfect. The helping verb **had** is the simple past form of "to have." A form of "to have" is required for the perfect tense. The action **cast** occurred earlier but is mentioned now.

18. *will be flying* — future progressive. **Will** is a helping verb that points to the future. The helping verb **be** is a form of "to be." A form of "to be" is needed for the progressive tense. The word **tomorrow** signals the future. **Will be flying** shows that the action **flying** will be in process at some future time (**tomorrow**). According to the sentence, the subject **he** will be flying the plane at some point in the future (**to-morrow**) if the skies are clear.

19. *have been choosing* — present perfect progressive. The helping verb **have** is a form of the verb "to have." A form of "to have" is needed for the perfect tense. The helping verb **been** is a form of "to be." A form of "to be" is needed for the progressive tense. **Have been choosing** shows the action (**choosing**) began in the afternoon and is still in progress. The subject of the sentence **they** began choosing furniture in the afternoon and is still choosing furniture.

20. *had been buying* — past perfect progressive. The helping verb **had** is the past tense form of "to have." **Had** is required for the past perfect tense. The helping verb **been** is a form of "to be." A form of "to be" is required for

the perfect tense. **Had been buying** shows the action (**buying**) was in process at some point in the past and was completed because it was interrupted by another action (**the train arrived**). According to the sentence, the subject **you** should have bought the ticket before the train arrived.

REVIEW

Of the three topics discussed in this section, subject/verb agreement is the most important to understand thoroughly. Basically, it is a matter of matching up the subject of the sentence with its correct verb form. Many grammar textbooks refer to this as agreeing in both number and person. If this seems like a confusing concept, just remember that a singular subject must be used with a singular verb form; this is what is meant by agreeing in number. Additionally, if the subject is in the third person (it uses or can be replaced by the pronouns he, she, it, they), the verb must also be in the third person.

Understanding the difference between action and linking verbs will help you avoid the very common error of using an adverb to modify a linking verb. After all, how many times have you heard someone say, "I feel badly for him." You have undoubtedly heard this so often that the correct expression—I feel bad for him—sounds as if *it* was the incorrect statement. However, for any person such as yourself who wishes to advance in the business or academic world, it is essential to avoid these errors, even when speaking. Doing so sets you apart as an educated person. If you are challenged by someone who believes that he/she is correct, you can gain respect and self-confidence by politely explaining the concept of linking verbs and predicate adjectives!

Correct use of verb tenses is important mostly for clarity. Since tense relates the time frame in which an action takes place, using the tense which is specific to the situation can help you avoid confusion. For example, if you are asked how long you have been preparing for an exam, consider the difference between the following responses:

I studied last week.

I have been studying since last October.

The first answer implies that your study efforts have been limited to the past week, while the second response indicates the entire scope of your preparation. Quite a difference!

Subject and Verb Agreement

WRITING

SUBJECT AND VERB AGREEMENT

IDENTIFYING SUBJECTS AND VERBS

All grammatical errors can be traced to a misunderstanding of the subject and verb in a sentence. The subject of a sentence is the person or thing who performs the action; the verb is the action word. In the following sentence, see if you can find the subject and the verb.

Kendra watches television.

Kendra is the subject and *watches* is the verb. Both the subject and verb are easy to locate because this sentence is simple.

Multi-word and Compound Subjects

Subjects often contain more than one word. Consider the following sentences in which the multiple-word subjects are underlined.

The three women carried umbrellas to the bus.

My retired father lives on a fixed income.

Sometimes there is more than one person or thing performing the action. In that case, the sentence has a **compound subject**.

Ben and Daniel are the co-captains.

Dogs and cats are popular house pets.

Pronouns as Subjects

Pronouns are often the subjects of a sentence. Pronouns are words which stand in place of nouns. In other words, they are a shortcut to writing the entire noun. In the following sentences, the word in parentheses is the pronoun which could replace the noun or nouns in the sentence.

My father works downtown.
(He)

Perri and Jamie went to the movies.
(They)

My family and I vacation at the shore.
(We)

Helping Verbs

Verbs may also require several words to express a particular action. These extra words are called **helping verbs**. *Should, will, may, could, would,* and *do* help express different ideas about the action. You must be able to recognize all the parts of the verb in order to make sure the subject and verb in a sentence agree. In the following sentences, the entire verb has been underlined for you.

She will go to school on Monday.

The dog was hurt in an accident.

On Saturday, we will be playing soccer.

Finding the Subject

Sometimes the subject of the sentence is difficult to identify. Remember, the subject is not necessarily the first word in a sentence; it is the person or thing that the sentence is based upon.

In the following sentences, the subject has been underlined for you. Ask yourself if you can see how the underlined word is the subject; notice how the subject either performs the action or is simply what the sentence is about. See if you can find the subject more easily by rephrasing the sentence without changing its meaning. The explanations below the examples demonstrate how you can find the subject.

What a great movie <u>"The Fugitive"</u> was!

Which word, exactly, contains the point of this sentence? If you guessed "movie," you were incorrect because the sentence isn't about any movie; it is about a particular movie called "The Fugitive." You could actually rephrase this sentence without changing its meaning at all to read

<u>"The Fugitive"</u> was a great movie!

Now it is more clear that "The Fugitive" is the subject of the sentence.

Does the <u>soup</u> taste good?

Questions such as the sentence above can be confusing unless you turn them into statements. Rephrase this question to make it a simple statement.

The <u>soup</u> tastes good.

Since the sentence is concerned with the soup, "soup" is the subject of the sentence.

Finally, the <u>train</u> arrived.

Often, sentences contain modifiers which add more detail. Do not let these additional words confuse you. If you strip away any unnecessary words, the basic sentence will read

The <u>train</u> arrived.

Since the train is performing the action — it is what is arriving — "train" is the subject of the sentence.

From out of the blue, came my great <u>idea</u>.

This sentence is complicated. It requires you to decide which word the sentence is based upon. The phrase "from out of the blue" describes the verb "came." It tells us when the idea came. The words "my" and "great" describe the word "idea." By process of elimination, you can see that the word "idea" is the subject. Rephrase the sentence and you can see this more clearly.

My great <u>idea</u> came out of the blue.

<u>Claire</u> and <u>Neil</u> are planning a great wedding.

In this sentence, it is easy to see that two people are doing an action. Both Claire and Neil are planning a wedding. If you ask yourself who is performing the action, it is simple to see that the subject is "Claire and Neil."

To review, any of the following techniques can help you find the subject of a sentence.

1. Rephrase the sentence, particularly if it is a question.

2. Try to determine what or who is doing the action.

3. If there is no action in the sentence, try to determine what the sentence is about.

4. Use process of elimination to find the subject.

Questions

Underline the subject of each sentence once. Circle the verb.

1. Mom and I went shopping early.

2. Wasn't Elizabeth great in the show?

3. They helped Gregory with his resume.

4. He and I went to the meeting.

5. Relationships involve commitment.

6. Those girls have long hair.

7. Did Felipe bring his sister?

8. The army was sent to Somalia.

9. Mrs. Chin grew vegetables.

10. The test will be given on Wednesday.

Answers

1. subject: Mom and I; verb: went shopping

2. subject: Elizabeth; verb: was

3. subject: They; verb: helped

4. subject: He and I; verb; went

5. subject: relationships; verb: involve

6. subject: girls; verb: have

7. subject: Felipe; verb: bring

8. subject: army; verb: was sent

9. subject: Mrs. Chin; verb: grew

10. subject: test; verb: will be given

AGREEMENT

Now that you have learned to find the subject and the verb in a sentence, it is essential that they agree. By agreement, we mean that a singular subject must have a singular verb. A plural subject must have a plural verb.

Consider the following sentence:

All the residents, including John, hopes Clinton wins.

Residents is the subject of the sentence. The phrase, *including John*, is an interruption. If you temporarily eliminate it, you can see that *the residents...hopes* is incorrect, since *residents* is a plural subject and *hopes* is a singular verb. Therefore, the sentence should be rewritten this way:

All the residents, including John, hope Clinton wins.

Prepositional Phrases

Sometimes a prepositional phrase confuses our ability to tell if a subject is singular or plural. A prepositional phrase is used to indicate the location or function of a noun. Prepositions are details which enhance your understanding of the subject, but can really make subject and verb agreement difficult. In the following sentences, the prepositional phrases have been underlined for you.

A trio <u>of musicians</u> is performing tonight.

A pair <u>of boys</u> is figure skating.

The home <u>of my ancestors</u> is burning to the ground.

Use the following strategy to help you identify the subject of a sentence and to determine if it agrees with the verb. Temporarily cross out all prepositional phrases. In the following sentences, it is much easier to see that the subjects and the verbs agree.

> A trio is performing tonight.
>
> A pair is figure skating.
>
> The home is burning to the ground.

Compound Subjects

Some sentences have a compound subject. All this means is that the subject consists of more than one word. In the sentence, "Reggae and calypso are Caribbean musical styles," the sentence is about two types of music: reggae and calypso. Both types of music, however, are considered together as the subject of the sentence. Therefore, the subject is plural and needs a plural form of the verb.

Sometimes substituting a pronoun will make it easier to tell if the subject is compound, and therefore, plural:

> Julio and Maria need a new printer for their computer.
>
> They need a new printer for their computer.

Sometimes compound subjects are connected by the words *either . . . or* or *neither . . . nor*. When these expressions are used, they show that a choice is being made. In the sentence "<u>Either</u> Lynda <u>or</u> Meryl can attend," it is clear that a decision has to be made: Lynda can go, or Meryl can go, but not both. In the sentence, "<u>Neither</u> Josh <u>nor</u> Jake came to the party," it is understood that of two potential party-goers, neither one came to the party. The result of using *either...or* and *neither . . . nor* is a singular subject, even though two people or places have been mentioned. This can be seen more easily when the sentences are broken down into two separate sentences.

> <u>Either</u> Lynda <u>or</u> Meryl can attend.

This is the same as saying:

> Lynda can attend. Meryl can attend.
>
> <u>Neither</u> Josh <u>nor</u> Jake came to the party.

Which is the same as saying:

> Josh did not come to the party. Jake did not come to the party.

When you are faced with a sentence using either of these phrases, substitute the phrase *either one* or *neither one* for the compound subject.

> <u>Either</u> the principal <u>or</u> the coach usually attends the game.
>
> <u>Either one</u> attends the game.
>
> <u>Neither</u> Nelly <u>nor</u> Patricia has enough money to go.
>
> <u>Neither one</u> has enough money to go.

If one part of the compound subject is singular and the other part is plural, make the verb agree with the subject which is closest to it.

> <u>Either</u> Joey <u>or</u> the boys <u>have</u> the tickets.

Joey is obviously one person, so *Joey* is a singular subject. *The boys* is clearly a plural subject. Since the plural subject is closer to the verb than the singular subject, the verb agrees with *the boys*, rather than *Joey*.

> <u>Either</u> the boys <u>or</u> Joey <u>has</u> the tickets.

When the position of the subjects is reversed, the singular subject *Joey* is now closer to the verb. Notice how the verb changes from *have* to *has* in order to agree with the subject. The same situation can be seen in the following pair of sentences:

> <u>Neither</u> the Gordons <u>nor</u> Sheryl <u>is</u> here.
>
> <u>Neither</u> Sheryl <u>nor</u> the Gordons <u>are</u> here.

☞ Practice: Subject and Verb Agreement

DIRECTIONS: Choose the verb in each sentence which agrees with the subject.

1. Several houses on our block (is, are) for sale.

2. This group of skiers (gives, give) lessons to beginners.

3. The chances for a win (is, are) good.

4. This pair of gloves (look, looks) like yours.

5. The footprints in this cave (seem, seems) very large.

6. This set of books (need, needs) to be returned to the library.

7. One of my favorite programs (begins, begin) at eight.

8. The lake near the cabins (were, was) deep.

9. The paper on the walls (was, were) washable.

10. The last box of toys (have, has) our name on it.

11. Both of the ladies (has, have) a meeting at two.

12. Two motors (are, is) running.

13. Two of the plants (are, is) dying.

14. The rungs of the ladder (was, were) loose.

15. Terri and Bernard (works, work) at the mall.

16. Each of the staff members (was, were) going to stay late.

17. The bag of grapes (is, are) next to the nectarines.

18. This kind of cookie (is, are) my favorite.

19. Both of his ears (are, is) red from the cold.

20. One of the secretaries (was, were) faxing the letter.

Answers

1. are. The subject of the sentence is **houses** (plural). A plural subject must have a plural verb (**are**). **On our block** is the prepositional phrase. The prepositional phrase comes between the subject and the verb.

2. gives. The subject of the sentence is **group** (singular). A singular subject must have a singular verb (**gives**). **Of skiers** is the prepositional phrase. The prepositional phrase comes between the subject and the verb.

3. are. The subject of the sentences is **chances** (plural). A plural subject must have a plural verb (**are**). **For a win** is the prepositional phrase. The prepositional phrase comes between the subject and the verb.

4. looks. The subject of the sentence is **pair** (singular). A singular subject must have a singular verb (**looks**). **Of gloves** is the prepositional phrase. The prepositional phrase comes between the subject and the verb.

5. seem. The subject of the sentence is **footprints** (plural). A plural subject must have a plural verb (**seem**). **In this cave** is the prepo-

sitional phrase. The prepositional phrase comes between the subject and the verb.

6. needs. The subject of the sentence is **set** (singular). A singular subject must have a singular verb (**needs**). **Of books** is a prepositional phrase. The prepositional phrase comes between the subject and the verb.

7. begins. The subject of the sentence is **one** (singular). A singular subject must have a singular verb (**begins**). **Of my favorite programs** is a prepositional phrase. The prepositional phrase comes between the subject and the verb.

8. was. The subject of the sentence is **lake** (singular). A singular subject must have a singular verb (**was**). **Near the cabins** is a prepositional phrase. The prepositional phrase comes between the subject and the verb.

9. was. The subject of the sentence is **paper** (singular). A singular subject must have a singular verb (**was**). **On the walls** is a prepositional phrase. The prepositional phrase comes between the subject and the verb.

10. has. The subject of the sentence is **box** (singular). A singular subject must have a singular verb (**has**). **Of toys** is a prepositional phrase. The prepositional phrase comes between the subject and the verb.

11. have. The subject of the sentence is **both** (plural). A plural subject must have a plural verb (**have**). **Of the ladies** is a prepositional phrase. The prepositional phrase comes between the subject and the verb.

12. are. The subject of the sentence is **motors** (plural). A plural subject must have a plural verb (**are**).

13. are. The subject of the sentence is **two** (plural). A plural subject must have a plural verb (**are**). **Of the plants** is a prepositional phrase. The prepositional phrase comes between the subject and the verb.

14. were. The subject of the sentence is **rungs** (plural). A plural subject must have a plural verb (**were**). **Of the ladder** is a prepositional phrase. The prepositional phrase comes between the subject and the verb.

15. work. The subject of the sentence is **Terri and Bernard** (plural). A plural subject must have a plural verb (**work**).

16. was. The subject of the sentence is **each** (singular). A singular subject must have a singular verb (**was**). **Of the staff members** is a prepositional phrase. The prepositional phrase comes between the subject and the verb.

17. is. The subject of the sentence is **bag** (singular). A singular subject must have a singular verb (**is**). **Of grapes** is a prepositional phrase. The prepositional phrase comes between the subject and the verb.

18. is. The subject of the sentence is **kind** (singular). A singular subject must have a singular verb (**is**). **Of cookies** is a prepositional phase. The prepositional phrase comes between the subject and the verb.

19. are. The subject of the sentence is **both** (plural). A plural subject must have a plural verb (**are**). **Of his ears** is the prepositional phrase. The prepositional phrase comes between the subject and the verb.

20. was. The subject of the sentence is **one** (singular). A singular subject must have a singular verb (**was**). **Of the secretaries** is a prepositional phrase. The prepositional phrase comes between the subject and the verb.

REVIEW

The best way to make sure the subject and verb agree is to be certain you have correctly located the subject. Remember that the subject isn't necessarily the first word in a sentence; it may not even occur at the beginning of the sentence. Rather, the subject is the word for the person or thing that the sentence is based upon.

Sometimes confusion arises about whether a subject is singular or plural. Often this issue is made obscure by the prepositional phrase. When the subject is singular, but the prepositional phrase is plural, most people are confused about which verb form to use. For example, in the sentence, "A bowl of apples was placed on the kitchen counter," the subject, "bowl," is singular. However, the prepositional phrase, "of apples," is plural. Since the subject is singular, regardless of the plural prepositional phrase which modifies it, the verb must be in its singular form. Therefore, the singular verb form, "was," has been used instead of the plural form, "were."

In sentences with a compound subject, decide if both subjects are uniformly singular or plural. If they are both one or the other, the verb choice is obvious. If, however, one subject is singular and the other is plural, then match the verb to the subject which is closest to it in the sentence.

Subject/verb agreement is an important, yet simple topic to master. Careful proofreading will point out any errors you may have inadvertently made when writing in a hurry.

Nouns

WRITING

NOUNS

COMMON AND PROPER NOUNS

A noun is a person, place, or thing. Any noun can be the subject of a sentence; all sentence subjects are either nouns or pronouns. All nouns are either common nouns or proper nouns. Common nouns are the names of people, places, or things in general. Words such as *kite*, *aunt*, *beach*, *dog*, *ice cream*, *friendship*, *emotion*, etc. are examples of common nouns. Proper nouns are specific names of people, places, or things. They are always capitalized. Names such as *Puerto Rico*, *Aunt Bessie*, *The World Trade Center*, *September*, etc. are examples of proper nouns.

common noun:	*month*
common noun:	*aunt*
proper noun:	*September*
proper noun:	*Aunt Bessie*

In the paragraph below, underline all the nouns and label them either common or proper.

Questions

At work today, I received a message that my cousins, Janie and Henry, were arriving at LaGuardia from Ohio on the 4:00 flight. I was flooded with conflicting emotions: excitement and panic. I was thrilled that they were coming, but was there enough food in the refrigerator and enough clean linens in the closet? I finally got myself under control, grabbed a taxi, and left for the airport.

Answers

work, message, cousins — common; Janie, Henry, LaGuardia, Ohio — proper; flight, emotions, excitement, panic — common; food, refrigerator, linens, closet — common; control, taxi, airport — common

FORMING THE PLURAL OF NOUNS

There are several rules for making singular nouns plural. The usual way is simply to add "s" to the end of a word.

Singular	Plural
desk	desks
book	books
girl	girls
guest	guests
lamp	lamps
letter	letters
idea	ideas
smile	smiles
cow	cows

However, there are many exceptions to this guideline. When a noun ends in a consonant followed by the letter "y," the plural is formed by changing the "y" to "i," and adding "es."

Singular	Plural
forty	forties
lady	ladies
baby	babies
country	countries
berry	berries
fairy	fairies
category	categories
sky	skies
secretary	secretaries

Questions

1. If the noun ends in a vowel followed by the letter "y," the plural is formed by adding "s." The first three have been done for you. Complete the remainder.

Singular	Plural
attorney	attorneys
guy	guys
valley	valleys
boy	
monkey	
buy	

2. If the noun ends in "s," "sh," "z," "ch," "sh," or "x," then add "es" to form the plural. Study how the first three were done, then complete the remainder yourself.

Singular	Plural
box	boxes
kiss	kisses
branch	branches
class	
ranch	
match	
fox	
dish	
waltz	

3. Many nouns are irregular and do not follow any rule. Memorize these plurals. If you are unsure how to form the plural of the ones left blank, look up the singular form in a dictionary. The plural form will be listed as well.

Singular	Plural
child	children
deer	deer
man	men
foot	
mouse	
sheep	
goose	
ox	
tomato	
tooth	
woman	
potato	

Answers

1.	boys	monkeys	buys
2.	classes	ranches	matches
	foxes	dishes	waltzes
3.	feet	mice	sheep
	geese	oxen	tomatoes
	teeth	women	potatoes

Often the final "fe" or "f" in one-syllable words becomes "ves."

Singular	Plural
half	halves
wife	wives
life	lives
leaf	leaves
hoof	hooves
calf	calves

However, if the "ch" is pronounced like "k," only "s" is added.

Singular	Plural
stomach	stomachs
monarch	monarchs

DIFFERENT TYPES OF NOUNS

Collective Nouns

A collective noun names a group of people, of places, or of things. Even though a group consists of many things, not just one, a collective noun is considered as a single unit; therefore it is singular. In the sentence, "Steven served on a jury," *jury* is a collective noun. We all know that a jury consists of 12 people, but when those 12 people are part of the jury, they are considered together as a unit. Since they are considered singular, they require a singular form of a verb.

The <u>panel</u> consists of six local ministers.
singular   singular
subject   verb

The following words are also collective nouns. Notice how they each consist of a group of members.

company	team
family	unit
committee	orchestra
army	group

Non-Countable Nouns

Since a noun is a person, place, or thing, you would naturally assume that you could count how many persons, places, or things you were dealing with. While it is certainly true that you can count toys, giraffes, bananas, or states, there are nouns which are impossible to count. Nouns which name ideas or emotions, for example, cannot be counted. Words like *love, friendship, chaos, anger, delight*, etc. are examples of these kinds of words. There are two other types of nouns which cannot be counted unless you divide them into units. While you can't count *milk, hair*, or *gold*, you can count *glasses of milk, strands of hair*, or *bars of gold*.

Non-countable nouns, like collective nouns, are also considered singular, never plural. Therefore, they are always used with a singular noun.

<u>Courage</u> <u>is</u> necessary for people in law
  singular   singular
  subject   verb

enforcement jobs.

Beautiful <u>hair</u> <u>is</u> a wonderful asset.
       singular singular
       subject   verb

Questions

Pick the correct verb to match the subjects in the following sentences.

1. The company (select, selects) its winning team.

2. The army (sets, set) up its tents.

3. Strength (are, is) required to enter the contest.

4. Gold (is, are) more valuable than silver.

5. Time (was, were) running out.

Answers

1. selects. **Company** is the subject. **Company** is a collective noun. A collective noun is considered singular and requires a singular verb (**selects**).

2. sets. **Army** is the subject. **Army** is a collective noun. A collective noun is considered singular and requires a singular verb (**sets**).

3. is. **Strength** is the subject. **Strength** is a non-countable noun. A non-countable noun is considered singular and requires a singular verb (**is**).

4. is. **Gold** is the subject. **Gold** is a non-countable noun. A non-countable noun is con-sidered singular and requires a singular verb (**is**).

5. was. **Time** is the subject. **Time** is a non-countable noun. A non-countable noun is considered singular and requires a singular verb (**was**).

Possessive Nouns

People, places, or things can have other things that belong to them. A dog has a tail, a country has a flag, a student has a bookbag, and Harold might have a snowmobile or a business. When a person, place, or thing owns something, to show possession the noun then must be written as a possessive noun. The following rules explain how to change the way a common or proper noun should be rewritten in order for it to become a possessive noun.

Rule: If the noun is singular, add " 's."

Harold has a new snowmobile.

<u>Harold's</u> new snowmobile is purple.

The dog has fleas.

The <u>dog's</u> fleas are bothering him.

Minnesota has beautiful lakes.

<u>Minnesota's</u> lakes are cold.

Rule: If the noun is plural and ends in the letter "s," just add an apostrophe to make it possessive.

The girls have a test Friday.

The <u>girls'</u> test will be difficult.

Secretaries have responsible jobs.

<u>Secretaries'</u> jobs are important.

Parents need to take more control.

<u>Parents'</u> committees will be formed to discuss this.

Rule: If the noun is plural, but does not end in "s," add an apostrophe and the letter "s."

Men wear sweaters.

<u>Men's</u> sweaters are on the first floor.

Children should have household chores.

<u>Children's</u> chores shouldn't be too demanding.

Love has certain hazards.

<u>Love's</u> hazards are worthwhile.

Rewrite the following sentences to make the nouns possessive.

Questions

1. James has a gray suit.

2. The president has a new advisor.

3. The pitcher has a difficult job.

4. The rays of the sun can be dangerous.

5. The Jones have a family car and it needs new tires.

6. My mother-in-law will visit next week.

7. The play had a dramatic ending.

8. The idea belongs to Susan.

9. The House of Representatives has a full calendar.

10. The Senate has a full calendar.

Answers

1. James' suit is gray. The sentence has been rewritten to show James owns the suit. **James** is a singular noun that ends in the letter "s." **James** becomes a possessive noun by adding an apostrophe after the letter "s" (**James'**).

2. The president's advisor is new. The sentence has been rewritten to show the president has an advisor. The noun **president** is singular. **President** becomes a possessive noun by adding an apostrophe and the letter "s" (**president's**).

3. The pitcher's job is difficult. The sentence has been rewritten to show the pitcher has a job. The noun **pitcher** is singular. **Pitcher** becomes a possessive noun by adding an apostrophe and the letter "s" (**pitcher's**).

4. The sun's rays can be dangerous. The sentence has been rewritten to show the sun has rays. The noun **sun** is singular. **Sun** becomes a possessive noun by adding an apostrophe and the letter "s" (**sun's**).

5. The Jones' family car needs new tires. The sentence has been rewritten to make a reference to the entire Jones family. **Jones** is a singular noun that ends in the letter "s." **Jones** becomes a possessive noun by adding an apostrophe after the letter "s" (**Jones'**).

6. My mother-in-law's visit will be next week. The sentence has been rewritten to show the mother-in-law has a visit. **Mother-in-law** is a singular noun. **Mother-in-law** becomes a possessive noun by adding an apostrophe and the letter "s" (**mother-in-law's**).

7. The play's ending is dramatic. The sentence has been rewritten to show the ending belongs to the play. **Play** is a singular noun. **Play** becomes possessive by adding an apostrophe and the letter "s" (**play's**).

8. It was Susan's idea. The sentence has been rewritten to show the idea belongs to Susan.

Susan is a singular noun. **Susan** becomes a possessive noun by adding an apostrophe and the letter "s" (**Susan's**).

9.   The House of Representatives' calendar is full. The sentence has been rewritten to show the House of Representatives has a calendar. **House of Representatives** is a singular noun that ends in the letter "s." **House of Representatives** becomes a possessive noun by adding an apostrophe after the letter "s" (**House of Representatives'**).

10.   The Senate's calendar is full. The sentence has been rewritten to show the Senate has a calendar. **Senate** is a singular noun. **Senate** becomes a possessive noun by adding an apostrophe and the letter "s" (**Senate's**).

☞ **Practice: Nouns**

> **DIRECTIONS:** Correct the errors in noun plurals, agreement with collective and noncountable nouns, and possessive nouns in the following sentences.

1.   Three woman waited in line for tickets to the Michael Bolton concert.

2.   My family are vacationing in Florida.

3.   In the fall, North Carolinas' mountains are beautiful.

4.   There are many desk in the classroom.

5.   The orchestra perform tonight at the Smith Civic Center.

6.   My fathers' trip to England has been postponed.

7.   During the wind storm, a branches fell from the maple tree.

8.   The milk smell sour.

9.   My bos's schedule is full next week.

10.   The peace treaty was signed by several countrys.

Answers

1.   **Woman** should be **women**. The word **three** signals a plural noun will follow. **Women** is a plural noun. **Woman** is incorrect because it is a singular noun.

2.   **Are** should be **is. Family** is a collective noun. A collective noun is considered singular and requires a singular verb (**is**). **Are** is incorrect because it is a plural verb.

3.   **North Carolinas'** should be **North Carolina's**. North Carolina becomes a possessive noun by adding an apostrophe and the letter "s" (**North Carolina's**). **North Carolinas'** is an incorrect possessive noun form of a word that is singular.

4.   **Desk** should be **desks**. The word **many** signals a plural noun will follow. **Desks** is a plural noun. **Desk** is incorrect because it is a singular noun.

5.   **Perform** should be **performs. Orchestra** is a collective noun. A collective noun is considered singular and requires a singular verb (**performs**). **Perform** is incorrect because it is a plural verb.

6.   **Fathers'** should be **father's**. The noun **father** becomes possessive by adding an apostrophe and the letter "s" (**father's**). **Fathers'** is an incorrect possessive noun plural form.

7.   **Branches** should be **branch**. The word **a** signals a singular noun will follow. **Branch** is

a singular noun. **Branches** is incorrect because it is a plural noun.

8.   **Smell** should be **smells**. **Milk** is a non-countable noun. A non-countable noun is considered singular and requires a singular verb (**smells**). **Smell** is incorrect because it is a plural verb.

9.   **Bos's** should be **boss'**. The boss has a schedule. **Boss** becomes a possessive noun by adding an apostrophe after the letter "s" (**boss'**). **Bos's** is an incorrect possessive noun form.

10.   **Countrys** should be **countries**. The word **several** signals a plural noun will follow (**countries**). The word **country** is made plural by changing the letter "y" to "i" and adding "es." **Countrys** is the incorrect plural form of the word **country**.

REVIEW

The following is a list of different types of nouns. Common nouns are easy to identify since they name ordinary objects, places, things, ideas, etc. Even easier to identify are proper nouns, since they are always capitalized and are always the *name* of a person or a place. Collective nouns name a group of people, places, or things that, although they may consist of more than one thing, are considered as one unit. They can only be identified by recognition. When a noun names an idea or an emotional feeling, it is called a non-countable noun, since it is not tangible; it cannot literally be counted. Also, when something is uncountable *unless* it is placed in a countable container, such as a glass of milk or a drop of rain, it is also a considered a non-countable noun. These types of nouns also can be identified only through recognition. Finally, possessive nouns are people, places, or things that have other things that belong to them. They are easily rec-

ognized by the apostrophe at the end of the word.

Common Nouns

boy	orange	hat
bench	giraffe	sock
pencil	picnic	car
flag	department	bed
basketball	money	bear

Proper Nouns

Minnesota	Lake Wobegon
Disney World	Delta Airlines
Grandpa Abe	Rabbi Platek
Uncle Tommy	China
Cape Canaveral	Toledo
Pastor Hernandez	Marxism

Collective Nouns

panel	family	team
army	company	corporation
group	unit	committee

Non-Countable Nouns

courage	love	joy
anger	hope	freedom
snow	despair	rain
idealism	happiness	pleasure
hair	milk	tyranny

Possessive Nouns

Jason's computer

America's economy

the *elephant's* memory

children's clothing

girls' dresses

the *college's* reputation

dogs' dishes

the *cat's* tail

angel's wings

Nouns are the least problematic part of speech. After all, all of you can recognize when something is being named. As you have seen, nouns undergo very little change in sentences; they are either singular or plural. Knowing how to form the plural of a noun is a matter of memorizing the few rules on the previous pages, but since the rules are fairly regular and uncomplicated, this should not prove too difficult. Similarly, learning how to form the possessive of a noun does not involve any complicated grammatical theory, just practice.

Writing

Pronouns

WRITING

PRONOUNS

TYPES OF PRONOUNS

Pronouns are the simple, everyday words used to refer to the people, places, or things (nouns) that have already been mentioned, or to indefinite people, places, or things. Pronouns usually replace nouns.

There are several kinds of pronouns. Personal pronouns take the place of a noun that names a person or thing. Subject pronouns are personal pronouns which are used as the subject of a sentence, while object pronouns are used as direct or indirect objects of the verb in a sentence. Possessive pronouns show ownership. (See the chart at the bottom of the page.)

Mr. Gilbert is a teacher.

He teaches high school.

The pronoun *he* replaces the previously mentioned *Mr. Gilbert. He* is the subject of the sentence, *he teaches high school.*

I am Alex.

Mrs. de la Cruz teaches me.

The pronoun *me* replaces Alex. *Me* is the object of the verb, *teaches.*

Mr. Katz is our teacher.

Mrs. Johannson is theirs.

The pronoun *our* replaces the names of all the people whom Mr. Katz teaches. The pronoun *theirs* takes the place of all the people whom Mrs. Johannson teaches. In both cases, possession is shown.

Here are some common pronoun errors:

Me and Daniel have seen that movie.

The subjects of the sentence are Daniel and the unnamed person whose name is replaced by the pronoun. Since the pronoun must therefore be a subject pronoun, and *me* is an object pronoun, it is incorrect to write *Me and Daniel.* The sentence should read as follows:

Daniel and I have seen that movie.

Last year the team elected both Emily and I.

The subject of this sentence is *team.* The objects of the verb "elected" are Emily and the unnamed person whose name is replaced by the pronoun. Since the pronoun therefore must be an object pronoun, and *I* is a subject pronoun,

Personal Pronouns			
	Subject	**Object**	**Possessive**
Singular	I, you, he, she, it	me, you, him, her, it	mine, yours, his, hers
Plural	we, you, they	us, you, them	ours, yours, theirs

it is incorrect to write *Emily and I*. Therefore, the sentence should read:

> Last year the team elected both Emily and <u>me</u>.

> Let's keep this a secret between you and <u>I</u>.

The word *between* is a preposition. Prepositions are always followed by their objects. In this sentence, the object will be an object pronoun, since the sentence already contains a pronoun, *I*. Since the pronoun *I* is a subject pronoun, it is always incorrect to write *between you and I*. The sentence should read:

> Let's keep this a secret between you and <u>me</u>.

Relative Pronouns

Relative pronouns play the part of subject or object in sentences and introduce groups of words (clauses) that act as adjectives. *What, who, whom, whose, which,* and *that* can be relative pronouns.

> The flower, <u>which</u> was yellow, made her smile.

> The girl <u>who</u> loved him lived down the block.

> I wonder <u>what</u> happened.

> Mrs. Friedman, <u>whom</u> I knew well, died suddenly.

> Darren, <u>whose</u> friendship I value, called yesterday.

> The class <u>that</u> Ben enjoys most is English.

Who is used as a subject and refers to people. *That* and *which* refer to non-human things; *that* is specific and *which* is general. *Whom* is used as an object and refers to people. *Whose* is used as a possessive pronoun.

Here are some common errors with relative pronouns:

> He is the boy <u>that</u> I love.

That refers to things, not people. The subject of this sentence is the personal pronoun *he*. The verb is *love*. The unnamed object of her love must be written as a relative object pronoun. Therefore, the sentence should read:

> He is the boy <u>whom</u> I love.

> Who's kidding <u>who</u>?

Who refers to the subject of the sentence. The verb *kidding* requires an object; therefore, it is incorrect to write *who* when an object pronoun is required. Instead, the sentence should read:

> Who's kidding <u>whom</u>?

> Calie, <u>who</u> I like a lot, is coming for dinner.

Since the verb *like* is an action verb, it requires an object. The word *who* is a relative <u>subject</u> pronoun. It must be replaced by a relative <u>object</u> pronoun. Therefore, the sentence should read:

> Calie, <u>whom</u> I like a lot, is coming for dinner.

> Morgan, <u>whom</u> is my friend, is coming for dinner.

The verb *is* is a linking verb. Linking verbs never have objects. In this sentence, the clause *is my friend* describes the subject, Morgan. Therefore, a relative subject pronoun must be used. The sentence should read:

> Morgan, <u>who</u> is my friend, is coming for dinner.

Indefinite Pronouns

This group of pronouns is so-called because the nouns they replace are indefinite.

Singular	Plural
everybody	few
somebody	both
anybody	many
nobody	several
everyone	others
someone	some
anyone	
no one	

The most common error made with indefinite pronouns involves making them agree with the remainder of the sentence.

> Everyone take out <u>their</u> pencil.

The subject *everyone* is singular, while the possessive pronoun *their* is plural; therefore, the subject and pronoun do not agree. The possessive pronoun must be made singular to agree with the subject.

> Everyone take out <u>his/her</u> pencil.

Reflexive Pronouns

These are the pronouns that end in "self" or "selves."

myself	yourself	yourselves
himself	herself	itself
ourselves	themselves	

Their main purpose is to reflect back on the subject of a sentence.

> She cut <u>herself</u>.
> (object, refers to *she*)

> I bought <u>myself</u> a new dress.
> (object, refers to *I*)

> You are just not <u>yourself</u> today.
> (object, refers to *you*)

> They consider <u>themselves</u> lucky.
> (object, refers to *they*)

> Give <u>yourself</u> a treat; go to the ice cream shop.
> (object, refers to *you* understood)

> After that dust storm I washed <u>myself</u> very well.
> (object, refers to *I*)

Reflexive pronouns also provide emphasis. When they serve this purpose, they then become intensive pronouns and should appear at the end of the sentence.

> We will triumph over this outrage <u>ourselves</u>.

> I will go to the ticket office <u>myself</u>.

> She will tell it to him <u>herself</u>.

> You must discover the meaning <u>yourself</u>.

> I suppose I will have to do it <u>myself</u>.

Errors to Avoid—Reflexive Pronouns

Do not use the reflexive in place of the shorter personal pronoun.

> NO: Both Darrin and <u>myself</u> plan to go.

> YES: Both Darrin and <u>I</u> plan to go.

> NO: <u>Yourself</u> will take on the challenges of college.

> YES: <u>You</u> will take on the challenges of college.

> NO: Either James or <u>yourself</u> will paint the mural.

> YES: Either James or <u>you</u> will paint the mural.

Watch out for careless use of the pronoun form.

NO: George <u>hisself</u> told me it was true.

YES: George <u>himself</u> told me it was true.

NO: They washed the car <u>theirselves</u>.

YES: They washed the car <u>themselves</u>.

Notice that the reflexive pronouns are not set off by commas.

NO: Mary, <u>herself</u>, gave him the diploma.

YES: Mary <u>herself</u> gave him the diploma.

NO: I will do it, <u>myself</u>.

YES: I will do it <u>myself</u>.

☞ Practice: Pronouns

> **DIRECTIONS:** Fill in the following sentences with a relative pronoun.

1. The woman, _____ is wearing red, is my aunt.

2. Leora seems upset. I wonder _____ awful thing happened.

3. The house, _____ had been destroyed by fire, had been abandoned.

4. The sweater _____ I borrowed from my sister got ruined.

5. The only kind _____ is available comes in white.

> **DIRECTIONS:** Choose the correct form of the pronouns given in parentheses.

6. Do not ask for (who, whom) the bell tolls!

7. If you know (who, whom) did it, please tell me.

8. The Knicks, (who, whom) are my favorite team, were NBA champions.

9. The car with (whom, which) I am most familiar has 4-wheel drive.

10. Was it she (who, whom) won the race?

11. Both of them gave (their, her) reports.

12. All the police officers must buy (his, their) uniforms.

13. Neither one of the boys forgot (his, their) books.

14. The clinic helps (us, we) whenever someone is sick.

15. Everyone should bring (their, his/her) trash to the curb.

> **DIRECTIONS:** In the following sentences, make the necessary corrections.

16. Both Ben and myself wish to welcome you.

17. They finished mowing the lawn theirselves.

18. He wrote the poem hisself.

19. Himself will return the videos.

20. Mr. Gregor, himself, went to court.

Answers

1. who. **Who** is a relative pronoun referring to a person (**woman**).

2. what. **What** is a relative pronoun referring to the unknown (**thing**).

3. which. **Which** is a relative pronoun referring to a non-human thing (**house**).

4. that. **That** is a relative pronoun referring to a non-human thing (**sweater**).

5. that. **That** is a relative pronoun referring to a non-human thing (**kind**).

6. whom. **Whom** is a relative pronoun. **Whom** is the object of the preposition **for**.

7. who. **Who** is a relative pronoun. **Who** is the subject of the clause **you did it** and refers to a person.

8. who. **Who** is a relative pronoun referring to people (**Knicks**).

9. which. **Which** is a relative pronoun referring to a non-human thing (**car**).

10. who. **Who** is a relative pronoun referring to a person (**she**).

11. their. **Their** is a possessive pronoun. A possessive pronoun shows ownership. The possessive pronoun **their** takes the place of the people's names referred to by **both** and shows these people own the reports.

12. their. **Their** is a possessive pronoun. A possessive pronoun shows ownership. **Their** takes the place of police officers and shows the police officers own the uniforms they wear.

13. his. **His** is a possessive pronoun. A possessive pronoun shows ownership. **His** takes the place of one and shows the books belong to neither one of the boys.

14. us. **Us** is an object pronoun. **Us** is the object of the verb **helps**.

15. his/her. **His/her** is a possessive pronoun. **His/her** takes the place of everyone and shows the trash belongs to everyone.

16. **Myself** is a reflexive pronoun. The reflexive pronoun refers back to the subject of the sentence. **Myself** is used incorrectly in this sentence. The correct pronoun is the subject pronoun **I**.

17. **Theirselves** is an incorrect pronoun form. The correct pronoun form is **themselves**.

18. **Hisself** is an incorrect pronoun form. The correct form is **himself**.

19. **Himself** is a reflexive pronoun. The reflexive pronoun refers to the subject of the sentence. **Himself** is used incorrectly in this sentence. The subject pronoun **he** is needed in this sentence.

20. **Himself** is a reflexive pronoun. A reflexive pronoun refers back to the subject of the sentence (**Mr. Gregor**). A reflexive pronoun is not set off by commas.

REVIEW

Pronouns fall into several categories, but the most important thing to know about them is that they replace nouns. A noun is an essential part of a sentence, since most subjects are nouns, but continually repeating the noun throughout the sentence or paragraph can become repetitious or even sound silly. Pronouns help us eliminate repetition by giving us a kind of shorthand replacement word. Furthermore, pronouns are always used to indicate a noun whose name or existence we are unsure of. When we ask, "Who is calling," we substitute the name of the unidentified caller with the pronoun "who." Imagine how complicated life without pronouns would be; when your son or daughter complains to you that "*everyone* else's parents lets them" do something you have forbidden, be grateful that the indefinite pronoun "everyone" has substituted a list of every single person your child knows!

Be on the lookout against using pronouns without clearly establishing the noun you are replacing. How often have you tried to follow a conversation in which the speaker continually refers to "he," or "she," or "them"? Don't you find yourself interrupting, "wait, *which* one said that," or " *who* did it?" Using an antecedent—just a fancy term for the noun which has been replaced by a pronoun—is the way to be sure your use of pronouns is clear and correct. Again, we cannot overemphasize careful proofreading. As you re-read what you have written, ask yourself if it is obvious to your reader what each pronoun refers to.

So many different words are pronouns that it is no wonder that studying them puts people off. Confronted with subcategories, such as possessive, relative, indefinite, subject, and object, many of you may feel as though you have wandered into dangerous territory, rife with opportunities to make mistakes. To help you put all this into perspective, remember that you do not have to memorize categories and lists of words that belong in them. All you really need to do is become familiar with the terms and develop a level of comfort with the logic behind the use of pronouns. Remember, all writers, even professionals, consult grammar books when they are unsure or confused about a potential mistake in their work. The point of this chapter is to familiarize you with the topic. Working on the exercises and reviews will help you use pronouns correctly.

Common Sentence Errors

WRITING

COMMON SENTENCE ERRORS

SENTENCE FRAGMENTS

Since a sentence is supposed to express a complete thought, a group of words that only expresses a segment of that thought is called a **sentence fragment**. Fragments usually occur when you are writing in a hurry and do not realize that what you have written is not a complete sentence. Usually, fragments can be easily found by simply reading over carefully what you have written. They can be fixed by adding whatever is missing — often just the subject or the verb. In the lines below, notice how the fragments have been made into correct sentences.

Fragment:
These employees who have worked so long.

Sentence:
These employees who have worked so long deserve a raise.

———————————

Fragment:
Pulled a tendon in his leg.

Sentence:
Elliot pulled a tendon in his leg.

———————————

Fragment:
Before the next inspection.

Sentence:
They cleaned up the lab before the next inspection.

The following may be either complete sentences or sentence fragments. Write S for each complete sentence and F for each fragment. Suggest a correction for the fragments.

Questions

1. After the rain stopped.

2. When I read, especially at night.

3. The salary you were offered seems fair.

4. Just for laughs.

5. I wish he would fix the dripping faucet.

Answers

1. F — We mowed the lawn after the rain stopped.

2. F — My eyes get tired when I read, especially at night.

3. S

4. F — Just for laughs, Geraldo pretended he failed the test.

5. S

RUN-ON SENTENCES

A run-on is a sentence with too much in it. It usually contains two complete sentences incorrectly separated by a comma, or two or more sentences that "run-on" meaninglessly. There are several ways to correct a run-on:

1. Separate the two complete sentences with an end mark. This is the simplest method to use, but it is not always the best way since it can produce short, choppy sentences if used too often.

    Run-on:
    You can transfer to Boston, you can transfer to Chicago.

    Correction:
    You can transfer to Boston. You can transfer to Chicago.

2. Instead of using an end mark, use a semicolon to connect the two complete sentences. This works well when the ideas in both parts of the run-on are closely related.

    Run-on:
    Talk softly, someone may hear you.

    Correction:
    Talk softly; someone may hear you.

3. Combine the two complete sentences with a comma and a conjunction (connecting word). This is often the best way to correct a run-on since it produces a logical connection between related ideas.

    Run-on:
    I eat ice cream, it makes me fat.

    Correction:
    I eat ice cream, but it makes me fat.

Correct the following run-on sentences. Answers may vary depending on which method you have chosen.

Questions

1. It was impossible to get through on the phone, the lines were down because of the storm.

2. Everyone knows who did it, no one is willing to talk.

3. I can't help worrying, Maleek has been gone for hours.

4. Feed the baby, she's been crying for five minutes.

5. We considered going to the movies, we wound up going bowling.

Answers

1. It was impossible to get through on the phone; the lines were down because of the storm.

2. Everyone knows who did it, but no one is willing to talk.

3. I can't help worrying; Maleek has been gone for hours.

4. Feed the baby. She's been crying for five minutes.

5. We considered going to the movies, yet we wound up going bowling.

PARALLEL STRUCTURE

When a sentence has compound parts, all the similar parts must be written in similar ways. This agreement in sentence structure is referred to as **parallel structure**. For example, if a sentence uses compound verbs, they must all be in the same tense and form. In a sentence with compound subjects, they must all be written in the same way. Lack of parallel structure is a common problem, but it is easily located by proofreading, and easily corrected by re-writing all the compound parts so that they match.

Incorrect:
In the summer I usually like swimming and to water-ski.

Correct:
In the summer I usually like swimming and water-skiing.

In the incorrect sentence the words *swimming* and *to water-ski* are not written in the same format. Changing *to water-ski* to *water-skiing* makes them agree. You could also have chosen to write *to swim* and *to water-ski*.

Incorrect:
Learning to write coherently, clearly, and with logic is the only way to learn.

Correct:
Learning to write coherently, clearly, and logically is the only way to learn.

The words *coherently* and *clearly* have been written as adverbs, while *with logic* has been written as a prepositional phrase. Changing *with logic* to *logically* makes all the compound parts of this sentence parallel by writing them all as adverbs.

Questions

Revise the following sentences to make the compound parts parallel.

1. My boss explained the cause, effect, and the results.

2. Our priest comforted us with seriousness and in a concerned voice.

3. The movie was interesting and had a lot of excitement.

4. The crowd pushed into the store, grabbed all the bargains, and were standing on long lines for the register.

5. Our company has reviewed your resume, checked your references, and the decision was made to hire you.

Answers

1. My boss explained the cause, effect, and results.

2. Our priest comforted us with seriousness and concern.

3. The movie was interesting and exciting.

4. The crowd pushed into the store, grabbed all the bargains, and stood on long lines for the register.

5. Our company has reviewed your resume, checked your references, and decided to hire you.

MISPLACED MODIFIERS

Often, a sentence contains a modifier, which is a word or a group of words which describe another word in a sentence. Modifiers can be one word, such as an adjective or an adverb. Sometimes, however, an entire phrase gives more detail about a particular word. If the modifier is not correctly placed as closely as possible to the word it describes, the sentence might not make sense.

Example:
Ari found five dollars eating lunch in the park.

The modifying phrase *eating lunch in the park* tells more about Ari, describing what he was doing. However, misplacing this phrase results in a rather silly sentence; it sounds as if the five dollars were eating lunch in the park, rather than Ari! The sentence should be corrected to read as follows:

While eating lunch in the park, Ari found five dollars.

or

Ari found five dollars while eating lunch in the park.

————

Example:
A package was sent to Stuart with many prizes.

The phrase *with many prizes* modifies the package, describing what it contains. However,

it was incorrectly placed next to the word *Stuart,* which implies that Stuart has many prizes, something that obviously doesn't make any sense. The sentence should read as follows:

A package with many prizes was sent to Stuart.

Questions

Rewrite the following sentences to correct the misplaced modifier.

1. He discovered a new route driving home.

2. I saw a circus caravan riding the bus this afternoon.

3. I read a book about primitive tribes flying to the Caribbean.

4. The clothing was given to the homeless in large packages.

5. We saw two girls riding bicycles from my window.

Answers

1. He discovered a new route while driving home.

2. While riding the bus this afternoon, I saw a circus caravan.

3. I read a book about primitive tribes while flying to the Caribbean.

4. The clothing was given in large packages to the homeless.

5. While looking from my window, I saw two girls riding bicycles.

☞ Practice: Common Errors

> **DIRECTIONS**: The following sentences contain errors in fragments, run-ons, parallel structure, and misplaced modifiers. Identify the error by writing F for fragment, RO for run-on, PS for parallel structure, and MM for misplaced modifier. Suggest a correction for the error.

1. Worked at the mall.

   _____

2. My sister loves pizza, she eats it everyday.

   _____

3. The restaurant serves Italian food, American food, and food from Greece.

   _____

4. I found a television show I liked changing channels.

   _____

5. The family who lives across the street.

   _____

6. I am searching for a new apartment, I hope to find one soon.

   _____

7. Susan drives slowly and with care.

   _____

8. Tom saw an automobile accident driving down the street.

   _____

9. Since the restaurant closed.

   _____

10. Albert considered attending a large university, he decided to attend a local community college instead.

   _____

Answers

1. (F) The fragment may be corrected by adding a subject, such as **he**. (**He worked at the mall**.)

2. (RO) The run-on may be corrected by adding a conjunction, such as **and**, after the comma.

3. (PS) The phrase **food from Greece** is not parallel with **Italian food** and **American food**. **Food from Greece** should be changed to **Greek food**.

4. (MM) **Changing channels** is a misplaced modifier. **Changing channels** should be placed before the subject **I** and set off with a comma.

5. (F) The fragment may be corrected by adding a verb. (**The family who lives across the street is from New Jersey**.)

6. (RO) The run-on may be corrected by deleting the comma and adding a semicolon.

7. (PS) **Slowly** is not parallel with the phrase **with care**. **With care** should be **carefully**.

8. (MM) The misplaced modifier **driving down the street** may be corrected by adding a subject (**while he was driving down the street**).

9. (F) The fragment may be corrected by adding a complete sentence and a comma after **closed**. (**Since the restaurant closed, we**

will have to find a new place to eat on Friday nights.)

10. (RO) The run-on may be corrected by deleting the comma and adding an end mark.

REVIEW

When you proofread, be on the lookout for the common sentencing errors discussed in this chapter. Sentence fragments are the simplest to find; they usually occur when your thoughts run faster than your pen. Simply add whatever was missing and the fragment becomes a sentence. When you spot a run-on sentence, either use the appropriate punctuation to fix it, or shorten the rambling sentence into shorter, more meaningful statements. Problems with parallel structure can be addressed by unifying the form of your compound words. Misplaced modifiers may be the most difficult sentence error to spot; read each sentence carefully and ask yourself as you read if the modifying phrase is located next to or near the word it modifies. If not, revise by repositioning the modifier.

Learning to recognize modifier phrases will be helpful. In general, modifiers such as simple adjectives or adverbs are not misplaced. Normally, in English syntax (the correct order of words in a sentence), the adjective is the word immediately before the noun it modifies. For instance, we say "the blue shirt," not "the shirt blue." Adverbs can appear either before or after the verb they modify, but in general

there is little difficulty finding them. The type of modifier that gives some people problems is the prepositional phrase, which functions in a sentence as either an adverb or an adjective. Consider the following sentences. The prepositional phrases have been underlined for you.

Michelangelo's statue of David is my favorite sculpture.

functions as an adjective

Chunks of ice hung from the tree's branches.

functions as an adjective

The lady with the black hair is my Aunt Selma.

functions as an adjective

In this photo, you can see how beautiful my home country is.

functions as an adverb

With their family's assistance, the young couple bought a car.

functions as an adverb

The baby was walking by 14 months.

functions as an adverb

Every prepositional phrase will modify either a verb or a noun in the sentence. Train yourself as you read to pick out the prepositional phrases and see if it is clear what word they modify. Then re-read the sentence to see if the modifier has been misplaced.

Modifying Words

WRITING

MODIFYING WORDS

ADJECTIVES AND ADVERBS

Adjectives and adverbs are modifying words. Modifiers help to make the meaning of a sentence clearer and more exact. It is one thing to say, "She wore a dress," but we get a much clearer picture when we modify the sentence with the following adjectives:

She wore a <u>tight-fitting black evening</u> dress.

Similarly, the sentence, "He smiled," makes perfect sense, but when we modify the sentence with an adverb, we can almost picture what is being described:

He smiled <u>very broadly</u>.

Adjectives and adverbs, therefore, "decorate" the basic sentence. They help us communicate more effectively by describing exactly what we mean.

Adjectives

An adjective is a word that describes a noun or pronoun. Adjectives answer one of the following questions:

How many?

Which one?

What kind?

In the sentences below, the adjectives have been underlined for you.

<u>Two</u> secretaries were hired.
(tells how many)

Angel bought a <u>green</u> sweater.
(tells what kind)

<u>This</u> is the movie I want to see.
(tells which one)

Mr. Turk gave me <u>some</u> instructions.
(tells how many)

Often, proper nouns (names of places or things) are used as adjectives.

We enjoy eating <u>Chinese</u> food.

Sonya enjoys <u>Latino</u> dancing.

They want to take a <u>Hawaiian</u> vacation.

Questions

Underline the adjectives in each sentence. Some sentences have more than one adjective. Note which question the adjective answers.

1. Fifteen runners finished the race.

2. These are the books I ordered.

3. The torn curtains have to be mended.

4. Battered cars rusted in the junkyard.

5. Bring me those papers over by the window.

6. Several cartons of food were donated to the homeless shelter.

7. Felicia wore a lovely Italian scarf.

8. Joachim is green with envy.

9. Few mushrooms were available.

10. Four stray dogs circled in the empty lot.

Answers

1. fifteen; how many

2. these; which one

3. torn; what kind

4. battered; what kind

5. those; which one

6. several; how many
   homeless; what kind

7. lovely, Italian; what kind

8. green; what kind

9. few; how many

10. four; how many
    stray, empty; what kind

Adverbs

An adverb is a word that describes a verb, an adjective, or another adverb. Adverbs are used to answer the following questions:

when?

where?

how?

to what extent?

In the sentences below, the adverbs have been underlined.

Shanikwa <u>quickly</u> finished her errands.
(tells how)

<u>Yesterday</u>, I began looking for a new job.
(tells when)

The lumber yard is <u>nearby</u>.
(tells where)

Manolo is an <u>extremely</u> attractive man.
(tells to what extent)

It is commonly assumed that all adverbs end in "ly." This is untrue. Adverbs that tell when or where something is done never end in "ly." These include the following adverbs: *never, today, also, somewhere, away, before, tomorrow, then,* etc.

An adverb may describe a verb.

Rachel <u>calmly</u> bandaged the injured patient.

Calmly is the adverb describing how the verb, *bandaged,* was done.

Joseph sang <u>softly</u> to the children.

Softly is the adverb describing how the verb, *sang,* was done.

An adverb can describe an adjective.

Michelle was <u>extremely</u> happy to hear from him.

Extremely is the adverb describing to what extent Michelle was happy. *Happy* is an adjective which describes Michelle.

An adverb can describe another adverb.

Rina spoke <u>too</u> softly to be heard.

Both *too* and *softly* are adverbs. *Too* describes to what extent Rina spoke softly. *Softly* describes how Rina spoke.

Questions

Underline the adverbs in the following sentences. Note which word the adverb describes and what question it answers.

1. The doctor has just left.

2. The extremely dry climate in the Southwest is good for asthma sufferers.

3. The newspaper was quite informative.

4. Grandma greeted us warmly.

5. Leora often talks to Morgan.

6. Lucy is looking for an apartment nearby.

7. Sidney is always on time.

8. Dr. Hernandez thoroughly examined her patient.

9. Peter drove over today.

10. We traveled everywhere.

Answers

1. just — tells when he left

2. extremely — tells to what extent it is dry

3. quite — tells to what extent it was informative

4. warmly — tells how she greeted

5. often — tells when she talks

6. nearby — tells where she is looking

7. always — tells when he is on time

8. thoroughly — tells how she examined

9. over — tells where he drove; today — tells when he drove

10. everywhere — tells where we traveled

CORRECT USAGE OF ADJECTIVES AND ADVERBS

The way to avoid making errors with adjectives and adverbs is to be certain what kind of word you are trying to describe. Since an adjective can only describe a noun or pronoun, it is always incorrect to use it with a verb.

Incorrect:
Don't take him serious!

Serious is an adjective, but in this sentence, it is describing the word *take*, which is a verb. Therefore, you should substitute an adverb for the adjective.

Correct:
Don't take him seriously.

Since linking verbs do not show action, but rather a state of being, they are used with adjectives, not adverbs. One of the most frequently heard errors is the following:

Incorrect:
Joanna feels badly about losing her glove.

In this sentence, *feels* is a linking verb, since it shows no action — Joanna isn't touching anything — it simply describes *how* Joanna feels. Since a linking verb can only be used with an adjective, it is correct to say:

Correct:
Joanna feels bad about losing her glove.

This error is so common that when someone uses an adjective with a linking verb, it may sound strange. However, it is correct. Do not intentionally make a grammatical error simply because you think it sounds strange to speak correctly.

Be aware that some words can be either adjectives or adverbs, depending on how they are used in a sentence.

Luis has a hard test to take.

In this sentence, *hard* is an adjective describing the noun *test*. It tells what kind of test Luis is taking.

Murray works hard.

In this sentence, *hard* is an adverb, describing the verb *works*. It tells how Murray works.

Using Adjectives and Adverbs to Compare

The comparative and superlative forms of adjectives and adverbs are used to compare two or more people, places, or actions.

When you compare two people, places, or actions, use the comparative form.

If the adjective or adverb can be pronounced in one syllable, form the comparative by adding "-er" to the end of the word. In adjectives ending with "y," the "y" changes to "i" before the ending is added.

Benjamin is <u>short</u>.

Ellen is <u>shorter</u> than Benjamin.

Marissa is <u>pretty</u>.

Olga is <u>prettier</u> than her cousin.

If the adjective or adverb consists of two or more syllables, put the words "more" or "less" in front of it.

Fran visits us <u>often</u>.

Gordon visits us <u>more</u> <u>often</u> than Fran does.

My little brother is <u>annoying</u>.

He is <u>less</u> <u>annoying</u> than Jackie's brother.

When you are comparing more than two people, places, or actions, use the superlative form of the adjective or adverb.

If the adjective or adverb can be pronounced in one syllable, add "-est" to the end of the word. With words that end in "y," remember to change the "y" to an "i" before adding "-est."

Henry is <u>short</u>.

Michael is the <u>shortest</u> of his brothers.

If the adjective or adverb consists of two or more syllables, put the words "most" or "least" in front of it.

Jerry is the <u>least</u> <u>active</u> member of the class.

Of everyone in the class, Janet finishes <u>most</u> <u>quickly</u>.

Never combine "-er" with *more* or *less,* or "-est" with *most* or *least.*

Incorrect:
This is the most ugliest painting I've ever seen.

Correct:
This is the ugliest painting I've ever seen.

Incorrect:
Diane is even more beautifuler than a movie star.

Correct:
Diane is even more beautiful than a movie star.

Irregular Comparatives and Superlatives

Not all adjectives and adverbs follow the pattern described above. Irregular adjectives and adverbs are formed by changing the words themselves. There is no way to learn the irregular forms except to memorize them. Fortunately, you are probably familiar with most of these forms.

Adjective/Adverb	Comparative	Superlative
good/well	better	best
many, much, some	more	most
bad	worse	worst
little	less	least
far	farther	farthest

The chart shown above contains the most commonly used irregular adjectives and adverbs.

☞ Practice: Adjective and Adverb Usage

> **DIRECTIONS:** Fill in the blanks with the correct form of the adjective or adverb in parentheses.

1. That is the _____ blouse I've ever seen. (pretty)

2. Mark is _____ than his brother. (tall)

3. Gregory is the _____ man in our department. (good)

4. The cake Aunt Grace baked is _____ than the one I made. (delicious)

5. A clown isn't always the _____ of people. (happy)

6. The mall is _____ from our house than the village. (far)

7. Calculus is _____ than geometry. (hard)

8. Fred is the _____ thought of man in our neighborhood. (high)

9. Today's weather is _____ than yesterday's. (bad)

10. He is the _____ demanding supervisor in our office. (little)

Answers

1. prettiest. **Prettiest** is an adjective modifying **blouse**. **Prettiest** is the superlative form of the adjective **pretty**. The superlative form ends in "-est." The superlative form compares more than two. **Prettiest** compares the blouse to all the other blouses seen.

2. taller. **Taller** is an adjective in the comparative form. The comparative form compares two people, places, or actions. The comparative form ends in "-er." **Taller** compares Mark's height to his brother's height.

3. best. **Best** is the superlative form of the adjective **good**. The sentence says that Gregory is the best man of all the people in the department.

4. more delicious. **Delicious** is made up of three syllables. The word **more** must be placed before **delicious** to indicate the comparative form.

5. happiest. **Happiest** is the superlative form of the word happy. The superlative form com-

pares more than two. The superlative form ends in "-est." **Happiest** compares the clown to the people.

6. farther. **Farther** is the comparative form of **far**. **Farther** compares the distance between two places: the distance between the mall and the house to the distance between the mall and the village.

7. harder. **Harder** is the comparative form of the adjective **hard**. The sentence compares the hardness of calculus to the hardness of geometry.

8. most highly. **Most highly** is the superlative form of **highly**. **Highly** is made up of two syllables. The word **most** must be placed before **highly** to indicate the comparative form.

9. worse. **Worse** is the comparative form of the adjective **bad**. The sentence compares today's weather to yesterday's weather.

10. least. **Least** is the superlative form of the adjective **little**. The sentence says that he is the least demanding supervisor of all the supervisors in the office.

REVIEW

A sentence without modifiers is like a window without a window treatment: bare and uninspiring. Modifying words such as adjectives and adverbs create mental images of what a writer wants us to see. Imaginative use of modifying words can help the reader visualize exactly what a writer intends. Consider the sentence, "Her new dress is blue." While the adjective "blue" gives us a general frame of reference for imagining what the dress looks like, it is not specific. The dress could be navy blue or pale turquoise. If, however, additional

adjectives, as well as adverbs are used, notice what a clearer image is created:

> Her new dress, blue as deepest midnight, flowed delicately behind her as she danced.

The adjectives "blue" and "deepest" describe the dress's color more accurately, while knowing that it is "new" suggests a freshness and excitement surrounding it. The adverb "delicately" tells more about how the dress flows, hinting that it is made of silk or chiffon. Accordingly, without modifying words, a vague image, rather than a concise one, is expressed.

Not only do modifying words help make ideas clearer, they also liven up our writing. Like the bare window, a sentence which lacks adjectives and adverbs is stark and often dull. In the lists below, some adjectives and adverbs have been grouped according to the senses they appeal to. Try incorporating them into your writing.

Adjectives that appeal to our sense of taste and smell

sweet	rancid	savory	aromatic
salty	peppery	sharp	perfumed
fishy	crisp	bitter	hot
burnt	sour	overripe	icy
moldy	spicy	fragrant	tangy

Adjectives that appeal to our sense of touch

slippery	mushy	woolly	velvety
gritty	feathery	damp	sticky
warm	fragile	crisp	oily
hot	steamy	boiling	leathery
thick	dry	waxy	satiny

Adjectives that appeal to our sense of sound

faint	loud	melodic	harmonious
hushed	deafening	earsplitting	noisy
piercing	inaudible	screaming	growling
still	roared	raucous	

Adjectives that appeal to our sense of sight

sheer	opaque	drab	pretty
radiant	regal	obese	bruised
blotched	patterned	flowery	grimy
tiny	huge	narrow	wide
handsome	wrinkled	youthful	muscular

Adverbs that describe movements

silently	hurriedly	smoothly
jerkily	precisely	swiftly
delicately	languidly	carefully
angrily	formally	sloppily
suavely	gracefully	awkwardly

Adjectives which describe colors

ruby red	*golden* yellow
midnight blue	*forest* green
dusky rose	*lemon* yellow
mint green	*icy* blue

A word of caution: many writers, thrilled with the vividness which modifiers add to their writing, tend to go overboard a little by overusing adjectives and adverbs. This can create sentences that are overwritten and, at times, silly. A good rule of thumb is to eliminate any modifiers that are not necessary to help make your sentence specific. Keep only those which establish the image you wish to create.

Punctuation

WRITING

PUNCTUATION

END MARKS

A **period** comes at the end of every sentence except for questions or exclamations.

Denise wore her red sweater.

Please take these forms to accounting.

A **question mark** comes at the end of a question.

Would you like me to check your coat?

Should the patient be moved so soon after surgery?

An **exclamation point** is used at the end of a sentence which is intended to show strong emotion, such as surprise, disbelief, or admiration. If it is used too often, it loses its impact. Therefore, use an exclamation point only when really needed.

I can't wait to see you!

Watch out for that car!

COMMAS

Because the comma has many different uses, it is often used incorrectly. In fact, it is the most frequently misused form of punctuation. The best way to avoid making errors is to learn the rules governing the use of the comma and to practice with the review drills.

Rule: Use a comma before a conjunction when you combine two or more simple sentences. Conjunctions are joining words, such as *and, but, for, nor, or, so, yet…*

1. Kiesha remained at home, <u>but</u> nobody showed up.

This sentence combines two simple sentences: *Kiesha remained at home* and *Nobody showed up.* The conjunction *but* shows the logical connection between the two sentences. It is now clearly understood that Kiesha stayed home to wait for some people, however, no one arrived.

2. Leah likes rock music, so we got her some CDs for her birthday.

In this sentence, two simple sentences, *Leah likes rock music* and *We got her some CDs for her birthday,* are combined. The conjunction *so* makes the logical connection, demonstrating that the reason for buying Leah the CDs for her birthday is that she likes rock music.

3. Debbie loves steak, yet she has trouble with cholesterol.

This sentence combines the simple sentence, *Debbie loves steak*, with another simple sentence, *She has trouble with cholesterol.* The conjunction *yet* shows a logical connection between the two; clearly her cholesterol makes her love of steak a problem.

Rule: Never use a comma to separate two complete sentences. The result is a run-on sentence, which is a common error in usage. You can test to see if both sentences are complete by replacing the comma with a period and capitalizing the first letter of the second sentence. If this looks correct, you know that the comma was incorrectly used.

Run-on:

I like coffee, he likes tea.

Comma replaced with period:

I like coffee. He likes tea.

See the section on the semicolon for other ways to avoid this error.

Rule: Do *not* use a comma before a conjunction when the sentence has a compound verb, unless the verb has more than three parts. A compound verb is simply two or more verbs in a sentence, connected by *and* or *or*.

Simone <u>roasted</u> a chicken and <u>tossed</u> a salad.

There are two compound verbs (*roasted*, *tossed*) in this sentence joined by the conjunction *and*. Therefore, no comma is needed.

Ewing <u>caught</u> the ball, <u>passed</u> it, and <u>ran</u> down court.

Since there are more than two compound verbs (*caught, passed, ran*) in this sentence joined by the conjunction *and*, a comma is needed.

Rule: Use commas on both sides of a phrase that interrupts the main part of a sentence. If the phrase can be removed from the sentence without changing its meaning, a comma is required.

You won't, <u>I suppose</u>, tell me who did it.

Sidney, <u>moreover</u>, hopes to take his vacation soon.

Linda, <u>my cousin from Toronto</u>, owns a book store.

Mrs. Peterson, <u>the lady I was telling you about</u>, is moving to another apartment.

Danny, <u>who works as a medical technician</u>, hopes to get his license soon.

In all the sentences above, the underlined phrases give extra detail, but can be removed without changing the basic meaning of the sentence.

Rule: Use a comma to set off the introductory word or words in a sentence. Notice how the introductory words don't change the basic meaning of the sentence.

<u>Yes</u>, I can have the proofs to you by tomorrow.

<u>In any case</u>, you will have to work late tonight.

Rule: Use a comma to separate two or more adjectives describing the same noun. However, if the adjectives must be written in a specific order, do not use a comma. In the following sentences, the adjectives have been underlined for you.

Our office is now using a <u>new</u>, <u>state-of-the-art</u> word processor.

Lottie's new dress is <u>short</u>, <u>black</u>, and <u>gorgeous</u>.

It seemed like <u>many exhausting</u> hours had passed before we could leave.

This job offers <u>certain excellent</u> benefits.

(Notice how the adjectives in the last two sentences must be written in this particular order in order to make sense. As a result, there is no comma.)

Another use for the comma is to separate items in a list.

When you go shopping, get me butter, eggs, milk, and juice.

My plans include getting some rest, working on my tan, and reading some good books.

Commas are also used with dates, to separate the day and the year, and with names of places, to separate a town and its state, or a city and its country.

Her graduation will be on June 22, 1998.

Beginning December 1, 1997, all employees will receive a raise.

I was born in Abilene, Texas.

Constanza comes from Athens, Greece.

Questions

Add or delete commas where necessary in the following sentences.

1. Mr. Ewing as a matter of fact was quite pleased with my progress.

2. Say have you seen my yellow shirt?

3. Juana my aunt is an excellent bookkeeper.

4. Enzo supervised the plans, and approved the job.

5. Pleased to be invited the boys wore their best suits.

6. The facts I guess will come out during the trial.

7. The baby turned rolled over and crawled to his mother.

8. This calculator has many, new features.

9. Marvin has some funny, new jokes to tell us.

10. The museum has a lovely authentic Renoir sketch.

Answers

1. Mr. Ewing, as a matter of fact, was quite pleased with my progress. Commas are needed around the phrase **as a matter of fact**. The

phrase interrupts the main part of the sentence.

2. Say, have you seen my yellow shirt? A comma is needed after the introductory word **say**.

3. Juana, my aunt, is an excellent bookkeeper. Commas are needed around the phrase **my aunt**. The phrase interrupts the main part of the sentence.

4. Enzo supervised the plans and approved the job. A comma is not needed after **plans**. The word group **approved the job** is not a simple sentence.

5. Pleased to be invited, the boys wore their best suits. A comma is needed after the introductory words **pleased to be invited**.

6. The facts, I guess, will come out during the trial. Commas are need around the phrase **I guess**. The phrase interrupts the main part of the sentence.

7. The baby turned, rolled over, and crawled to his mother. A comma is needed to separate items in a list (**turned, rolled over, and crawled**).

8. This calculator has many new features. A comma is not needed after the adjective **many**. **Many** must be placed before the adjective **new**; therefore, the comma is not needed.

9. Marvin has some funny new jokes to tell us. A comma is not needed after the adjective **funny**. **Funny** must be placed before the adjective **new**; therefore, the comma is not needed.

10. The museum has a lovely, authentic Renoir sketch. A comma is needed to separate the adjectives **lovely authentic**, which modify the phrase **Renoir sketch**.

SEMICOLONS AND COLONS

A semicolon [;] is used to separate two complete sentences that you wish to have read as one sentence because they are ideas which are somehow connected. It takes the place either of a period or of a comma and a conjunction.

My father is a Democrat; my mother is a Republican.

This sentence could also be written as follows:

My father is a Democrat. My mother is a Republican.

or

My father is a Democrat, but my mother is a Republican.

The colon [:] is always preceded by a complete sentence. It is never correct to write, *for example:* since *for example* is not a complete sentence. Instead, use a complete sentence before following a colon with a list.

I will need the following items from inventory: a ream of paper, staples, a hole punch, index cards, and a tape dispenser.

A colon, not a comma, is always used after the greeting in a business letter.

Dear Mr. O'Donnell:

not

Dear Mr. O'Donnell,

Questions

Add a semicolon and colon where needed.

1. My sister writes romance novels she published two novels last year.

2. I will need the following items for school next semester pens, pencils, composition books, computer disks, and notebook paper.

3. My husband and I ate dinner at the new Italian restaurant the food was terrible.

4. I plan to get my GED then I plan to attend college.

5. Dear Mr. Phillips

Answers

1. A semicolon [;] is needed to separate the two sentences. Sentence 1 is "My sister writes romance novels." Sentence 2 is "she published two novels last year."

2. A colon [:] is needed after the complete sentence "I will need the following items for school next semester." The list "pens, pencils, composition books, computer disks, and notebook paper" follows the colon.

3. A semicolon [;] is needed to separate the two sentences. Sentence 1 is "My husband and I ate dinner at the new Italian restaurant." Sentence 2 is "the food was terrible."

4. A semicolon [;] is needed to separate the two sentences. Sentence 1 is "I plan to get my GED." Sentence 2 is "then I plan to attend college."

5. A colon [:] is needed after the greeting in a business letter (Dear Mr. Phillips:).

QUOTATION MARKS

Quotation marks [" "] are most commonly used to indicate the exact words used by another speaker or a writer. Use them when you are writing dialogue, or when you are writing a research paper and need to quote someone else's words exactly.

When you are quoting dialogue, begin with a quotation mark and capitalize the first letter if you are quoting a complete sentence. After the appropriate end mark (a period, question mark, or exclamation mark), put another quotation mark.

> "Where have you been?" asked Mama.

> Wang Chiagang blamed his mistake on his sister, complaining, "She interrupted me three times!"

Use a comma before the last quotation mark if you are quoting a simple statement.

> "Yes, I'll marry you," said Yonina.

If you are writing a research paper and need to quote another writer's words exactly, use quotation marks to enclose the writer's exact words. If you wish to leave out some of the original words, use an ellipsis [...] to take the place of the missing words.

> In his most famous speech, Martin Luther King said, "I have a dream...."

> Carlos Baker, Ernest Hemingway's biographer, wrote that "life was boring for him after Paris."

Do not use quotation marks when you are indirectly quoting someone. When you quote indirectly, you are using your own words and therefore do not need quotation marks.

Quotation marks are also used when writing the titles of TV shows, poems, short stories, and book chapters. (Titles of books, motion pictures, newspapers, and magazines are underlined.)

> "MASH" was one of the country's most beloved TV shows.

> Keats wrote "Ode to a Grecian Urn."

> "Big Blonde" is a short story by Dorothy Parker.

> Our teacher assigned "Childhood Development," Chapter 18 in Human Behavior.

Questions

Rewrite the following sentences by inserting quotation marks where they are needed.

1. I just might come, said Mr. Sakura. What time does it start?

2. Three o'clock, I replied.

3. Mother and Son is one of Langston Hughes' best poems.

4. Are you planning to leave work early today? asked my boss.

5. Theodore Roosevelt said, The only man who makes no mistakes is the man who never does anything.

6. President Herbert Hoover promised Americans a chicken in every pot, but he fell short on his promise.

7. Read Another Country, is a short story by Hemingway.

8. Sesame Street helps children learn about numbers and the alphabet.

9. Alfred Lord Tennyson's Crossing the Bar is one of my favorite poems.

10. The directions stated, this toy is designed for children ages three and older.

Answers

1. Quotation marks are needed around Mr. Sakura's words "I just might come" and "What time does it start" "I" and "What" are capitalized because these words begin a direct quotation. A comma is needed after "come" because the word group is a complete sentence.

2. Quotation marks are needed around the speaker's words "Three o'clock." "Three" is capitalized because it begins a direct quotation.

3. Quotation marks are needed around the poem title "Mother and Son."

4. Quotation marks are needed around the boss' words "Are you planning to leave work early today?"

5. Quotation marks are needed around "The

only man who makes no mistakes is the man who never does anything."

6. Quotation marks are needed around Herbert Hoover's words "a chicken in every pot."

7. Quotation marks are needed around the short story title "Another Country."

8. Quotation marks are needed around the television show title "Sesame Street."

9. Quotation marks are needed around the poem title "Crossing the Bar."

10. Quotation marks are needed around the sentence "This toy is designed for ages three and older." "This" is capitalized because it begins a direct quotation.

☞ **Practice: Punctuation**

DIRECTIONS: Add correct punctuation where needed.

1. She wants a dozen bagels four plain two poppy two sesame two pumpernickel and two cinnamon raisin.

2. On December 3 1952 I was born in the Bronx New York.

3. By the end of the day there were only two things on her mind rest and relaxation.

4. Burgundy and maroon are very similar colors scarlet is altogether different.

5. Prepare the recipe as follows 1) slice the oranges thinly 2) arrange them in a ring around the strawberries 3) pour the liqueur over both fruits.

6. Only some of the women can join us Claire Sandy Cathy and Bonnie.

7. Music lightens life literature deepens it.

8. For a long time people thought men were superior to women even now it is not an easy attitude to overcome.

9. Dear Ms. Fielding

10. They were willing to accept the proposal he was not.

Answers

1. A colon [:] is needed after the complete sentence "She wants a dozen bagels." Commas are needed to separate items in the list "four plain, two poppy, two sesame, two pumpernickel, and two cinnamon raisin," which follows the colon.

2. A comma is needed between the date "December 3" and the year "1952." A comma is needed after the introductory phrase "On December 3, 1952." A comma is needed between "Bronx" and its state "New York."

3. A comma is needed after the introductory phrase "By the end of the day." A colon is needed after the complete sentence "By the end of the day there were only two things on her mind."

4. A semicolon [;] is needed to separate two sentences. Sentence 1 is "Burgundy and maroon are very similar colors." Sentence 2 is "scarlet is altogether different."

5. A colon [:] is needed after the complete sentence "Prepare the recipe as follows." Commas are needed to separate items in the list "1) slice the oranges thinly, 2) arrange them in a ring around the strawberries, and 3) pour the liqueur over both fruits," which follows the colon.

6. A colon [:] is needed after the complete sentence "Only some of the women can join us." Commas are needed to separate items in the list "Claire, Sandy, Cathy, and Bonnie," which follow the colon.

7. A semicolon [;] is needed to separate the two sentences. Sentence 1 is "Music lightens life." Sentence 2 is "literature deepens it."

8. A comma is needed after the introductory phrase "For a long time." A semicolon [;] is needed to separate the two sentences. Sentence 1 is " For a long time, people thought men were superior to women." Sentence 2 is "even now it is not an easy attitude to overcome."

9. A colon [:] is needed after the greeting of a business letter "Dear Ms. Fielding."

10. A semicolon [;] is needed to separate the two sentences. Sentence 1 is "They were willing to accept the proposal." Sentence 2 is "he was not."

REVIEW

Without punctuation, thoughts cannot be expressed clearly or logically. A sentence which lacks an end mark flows directly into the next sentence. Commas are crucial for separating main ideas from interruptions. Failure to use commas can radically change the meaning of a sentence, while quotation marks help us differentiate between the writer's words and those of someone he or she has quoted. As you work on the practice drills in this chapter, you will notice how confusing it is to read the sentences with incorrect punctuation. Therefore, mastering the basics of punctuation is a fundamental part of learning to write well.

You may have wondered why we did not include any instructions on the proper use of dashes and parentheses. While both forms of punctuation are valid, they are not always appropriate in formal writing situations. For the purpose of preparing for the GED exam, it is a good idea to reduce the instances in which you use dashes or parentheses.

The dash functions very much like a comma, colon, or semicolon.

Sara—always accustomed to the best— ordered caviar.

While dashes can be very useful, they tend to make your writing appear informal and "dashed" off; therefore, it is best not to use them in college or business writing. Parentheses contain brief explanations or interruptions.

They separate parts of a sentence in very much the same way an aside in a dramatic production separates what is being spoken to a character from what is being told to the audience. The only acceptable use for the parenthesis in formal writing is to indicate an item on another page of a memo, or as a reference to another page.

A shipment of 10,000 pounds of steel was delivered to Mendelsohn Productions (see attached delivery schedule).

One mistake many people make is to assume that the well-known advice to add a comma whenever you would take a breath is correct. It is not. As you study this book, make frequent reference to this chapter. Before long, using punctuation correctly will be second nature to you.

Writing

Capitalization

WRITING

CAPITALIZATION

When a letter is capitalized, it calls special attention to itself. This attention should be for a good reason. There are standard uses for capital letters as well as much difference of opinion as to what should and should not be capitalized. In general, capitalize 1) all proper nouns, 2) the first word of a sentence, and 3) a direct quotation.

NAMES OF SHIPS, AIRCRAFT, SPACECRAFT, AND TRAINS

Apollo 13

Mariner IV

DC-10

S. S. United States

Sputnik II

Boeing 707

NAMES OF DEITIES

God

Jupiter

Allah

Zeus

Buddha

Diana

Jehovah

Shiva

GEOLOGICAL PERIODS

Neolithic age

Cenozoic era

late Pleistocene times

Age of Reptiles

Tertiary period

NAMES OF ASTRONOMICAL BODIES

Venus

Big Dipper

the Milky Way

Halley's comet

Ursa Major

North Star

Scorpio

Deneb

the Crab Nebula

Pleiades

(Note that *sun, moon,* and *earth* are not capitalized unless they are used with other astronomical terms that are capitalized.)

PERSONIFICATIONS

Reliable **Nature** brought her promise of Spring.

Bring on **Melancholy** in his sad might.

Morning in the bowl of night has flung the stone/that set the stars to flight.

HISTORICAL PERIODS

the Middle Ages

World War I

Reign of Terror

Great Depression

Christian Era

Roaring Twenties

Age of Louis XIV

Renaissance

ORGANIZATIONS, ASSOCIATIONS, AND INSTITUTIONS

Girl Scouts of America

Kiwanis

Young Men's Christian Association

North Atlantic Treaty Organization

New York Yankees

League of Women Voters

Smithsonian Institution

Unitarian Church

the Library of Congress

Common Market

the Illinois Central

New York Philharmonic

Franklin Glen High School

GOVERNMENT AND JUDICIAL GROUPS

New Jersey City Council

Committee on Foreign Affairs

Senate

House of Commons

Arkansas Supreme Court

Parliament

Peace Corps

House of Representatives

Municipal Court of Chicago

Department of State

Census Bureau

Iowa Board of Education

United States Court of Appeals

A general term that accompanies a specific name is capitalized only if it follows the specific name. If it stands alone or comes before the specific name, it is put in lowercase.

Washington State

the state of Washington

Senator Dixon

the senator from Illinois

Central Park

the park

Golden Gate Bridge

the bridge

President Andrew Jackson

the president of the U.S.

Pope John XXIII

the pope

Queen Elizabeth I

the queen, Elizabeth I

Tropic of Capricorn

the tropics

Glen Brook High School

the high school in Glen Brook

Monroe Doctrine

the doctrine originated by Monroe

the Milky Way Galaxy

our galaxy, the Milky Way

the Mississippi River

the river

Easter Day

the day we celebrated Easter

Treaty of Versailles

the treaty signed at Versailles

Webster's Dictionary

a dictionary by Webster

Use a capital to start a sentence or a sentence fragment.

Our car would not start.

When will you leave? I need to know right away.

Never!

Let me in! Right now!

When a sentence appears within a sentence, start it with a capital.

The main question is, Where do we start?

We had only one concern: When would we eat?

My sister said, "I'll find the Monopoly set."

He answered, "We can only stay a few minutes."

In poetry, it is usual practice to capitalize the first word of each line even if the word comes in the middle of a sentence.

When I consider everything that grows
Holds in perfection but a little moment,
That this huge stage produceth naught
    but shows,
Whereon the stars in secret influence
    comment.
            —William Shakespeare

She dwells with Beauty—Beauty that
    must die;
And Joy, whose hand is ever at his lips
Bidding Adieu.
            —John Keats

The most important words of titles are capitalized. Those words not capitalized are conjunctions (e.g., *and, or, but*), articles (e.g., *a, the, an*), and short prepositions (e.g., *of, on, by, for*). The first and last word of a title must always be capitalized.

A Man for All Seasons

Crime and Punishment

Of Mice and Men

"Let Me In"

Rise of the West

"What to Look For"

"Sonata in G-Minor"

"The Ever-Expanding West"

Strange Life of Ivan Osokin

"Rubaiyat of Omar Khayyam"

"All in the Family"

"Symphony No. 41"

"Ode to Billy Joe"

"Piano Concerto No. 5"

☞ **Practice: Capitalization**

> **DIRECTIONS:** The following sentences contain errors in capitalization. Correct these sentences by making words capital where necessary, and other words lowercase where necessary.

1. Where is the crab Nebula?

2. The girl scouts of America sell delicious cookies.

3. This year, senator Burns will run for re-election.

4. Barbara said, "let me know when you are off the phone."

5. beth's new car is a black dodge daytona which she purchased at the dodge dealer in new york city.

6. mike and jackie are both graduates of edison high school.

7. glaciers from the ice age still exist.

8. Today in class, the Professor lectured on the Neolithic Age.

9. sergeant bruce whisman of the united states marine corps is stationed in hawaii.

10. We will be spending easter day with our aunt clara, who lives near the mississippi river.

11. Helen asked, "when will betty and Rich be returning from yellowstone park?"

12. our english teacher will be reviewing the first 20 pages of the book *of mice and men* with the class.

13. The case went as high as the United States court of appeals.

14. at the baseball game last night, the Los Angeles dodgers beat the New York yankees by Ten runs.

15. Eric asked the teacher, "do you have a Webster's dictionary?"

Answers

1. Where is the Crab Nebula? "Crab" should be capitalized. "Crab Nebula" is the name of an astronomical body. Names of astronomical bodies are capitalized.

2. The Girl Scouts of America sell delicious cookies. "Girls" and "Scouts" are capitalized. The Girl Scouts of America is the name of an organization. Names of organizations are capitalized.

3. This year, Senator Burns will run for re-election. "Senator" is capitalized. The general term "senator" is capitalized because it is followed by a specific person's name "Burns."

4. Barbara said, "Let me know when you are off the phone." "Let" is capitalized because it begins a direct quotation. The first word of a direct quotation is capitalized.

5. Beth's new car is a black Dodge Daytona

which she purchased at the Dodge dealer in New York City. "Beth" is capitalized. The first word of a sentence is capitalized. "Beth" is also a proper noun.

6.   Mike and Jackie are both graduates of Edison High School. "Mike" and "Jane" are capitalized because they are proper nouns, and they begin a sentence. "Edison High School" is capitalized because it is the name of an institution.

7.   Glaciers from the Ice Age still exist. "Glaciers" is capitalized because it begins a sentence. "Ice Age" is capitalized because it is a geological period.

8.   Today in class, the professor lectured on the Neolithic age. The general term "professor" should not be capitalized because it is not followed by a specific person's name. "Age" is not capitalized because it is not part of a geological period.

9.   Sergeant Bruce Whisman of the United States Marine Corps is stationed in Hawaii. "Bruce Whisman" is a proper name, so it is capitalized. "United States Marine Corps" is capitalized because it is a government group. "Hawaii" is capitalized because it is the name of a specific state.

10.   We will be spending Easter Day with our Aunt Clara, who lives near the Mississippi River. "Easter Day " is capitalized because it is the name of a specific holiday. "Aunt Clara" is capitalized because it is a proper noun. "Mississippi River" is capitalized because it is the name of a specific river.

11.   Helen asked, "When will Betty and Rich be returning from Yellowstone Park?" "When" is capitalized because it begins a direct quotation. The first word of a direct quotation is capitalized. "Betty" is capitalized because it is a proper noun. "Yellowstone Park" is capitalized because it is the name of a specific place.

12.   Our English teacher will be reviewing the first 20 pages of the book *Of Mice and Men* with the class. "English" is capitalized because it is the name of a specific course. The major words in the title *Of Mice and Men* are capitalized. *And* is not capitalized because it is a conjunction.

13.   The case went as high as the United States Court of Appeals. "Court of Appeals" is capitalized because it is the name of a judicial group. Names of judicial groups are capitalized.

14.   At the baseball game last night, the Los Angeles Dodgers beat the New York Yankees by ten runs. "Dodgers" and "Yankees" are capitalized. The Los Angeles Dodgers and the New York Yankees are organizations. Names of organizations are capitalized. "Ten" is not capitalized. Numbers are not capitalized.

15.   Eric asked the teacher, "Do you have a Webster's Dictionary?" "Do" is capitalized because it begins a direct quotation. The first word of a direct quotation is capitalized. *Webster's Dictionary* is capitalized because it is a title.

REVIEW

Remember, all proper nouns, the first word of a sentence, and a direct quotation should be capitalized. In general, the most important words of titles are capitalized.

Sentence Structure

WRITING

SENTENCE STRUCTURE

COMPOUND SENTENCES

In the previous chapter, you learned to use a comma when combining two or more simple sentences. When two or more simple sentences are joined together with a comma and a conjunction, the result is called a **compound sentence**.

Two simple sentences:
Margie wants to leave.
Her husband isn't ready.

Compound sentence:
Margie wants to leave, but her husband isn't ready.

It is good writing only if the simple sentences that make up a compound sentence are closely related. When you write quickly, you may accidently combine two sentences without showing any logical relationship between them. Proofread your writing carefully to make sure all your compound sentences make sense.

Gregory wants to go to the disco. He is only 18.

Gregory wants to go to the disco, <u>and</u> he is only 18.

There is no relationship between the two simple sentences joined above. By using a different conjunction, however, a logical connection can be made.

Gregory wants to go to the disco, <u>but</u> he is only 18.

Compound sentences are different from sentences with compound verbs. In a compound sentence, there are separate subjects and verbs, just as there were when the simple sentences were separate. In the example above, *Gregory* is the subject and *wants* is the verb in the first clause in the sentence (a <u>clause</u> is a group of words with a subject and a verb that does not express a complete thought). *He* is the

subject and *is* is the verb in the second clause of the sentence. Compare this to a sentence with a compound verb:

Gregory <u>played</u> basketball and <u>went</u> to school.

Even though there are two verbs, there is only one subject, *Gregory*. This is not a compound sentence because if it were broken down into two clauses, the second clause would have to "borrow" the subject from the first clause.

Gregory played basketball. [Gregory] went to school.

One way to tell if a sentence is compound is to break it into two clauses, as was done in the example above. If the two clauses minus the comma and the conjunction could be complete sentences on their own, the sentence is compound.

Questions

Use the conjunctions in parentheses to join the simple sentences into compound sentences.

1. I thought I knew the address. I forgot. (but)

2. Jim knows you are disappointed. He has been aware of this for a long time. (and)

3. Denise wants a better job. She started looking in the classified ads. (so)

4. *Nixon* was a fascinating film. It was too long to sit through in comfort. (yet)

5. Writing isn't always easy. It can be rewarding. (but)

6. Frannie did the shopping. Mark helped her with the cooking. (and)

7. She really dislikes exercising. She needs to tone her muscles. (but)

8. Trahn wants to become a U.S. citizen. He will take a citizenship class. (so)

9. Mary tried to improve her word processing skills. Employers are impressed by computer literacy. (for)

10. Martine speaks French. Guadeloupe speaks Spanish. (and)

Answers

1. I thought I knew the address, but I forgot.

2. Jim knows you are disappointed, and he has been aware of this for a long time.

3. Denise wants a better job, so she started looking in the classified ads.

4. *Nixon* was a fascinating film, yet it was too long to sit through in comfort.

5. Writing isn't always easy, but it can be rewarding.

6. Frannie did the shopping, and Mark helped her with the cooking.

7. She really dislikes exercising, but she needs to tone her muscles.

8. Trahn wants to become a U.S. citizen, so he will take a citizenship class.

9. Mary tried to improve her word processing skills, for employers are impressed by computer literacy.

10. Martine speaks French, and Guadeloupe speaks Spanish.

COMPLEX SENTENCES

Before you can understand what a complex sentence is, you need to know about main clauses and dependent clauses. A dependent clause is a group of words that contains a subject and a verb, but does not express a complete thought the way a sentence does. A main clause, however, *could* stand by itself as a sentence. When a complex sentence is split into two parts, there is at least one complete sentence (main clause) and another part (the dependent clause) that depends on the complete sentence in order to make sense. Sound confusing? The example below will illustrate this more clearly.

> Before we start class, we always say the Pledge of Allegiance.

Break the sentence down into its two parts, and you will get:

1. Before we start class

2. we always say the Pledge of Allegiance.

Part 1 makes no sense on its own. It is a sentence fragment because it does not express a complete thought. Part 2 does express a complete thought and needs only to have the first letter of the first word capitalized in order to stand on its own as a sentence. Therefore, Part 1 is a dependent clause and Part 2 is a main clause.

When writing complex sentences, be aware that the dependent clause can be placed in front of the main clause, behind it, or in the middle. The dependent clauses in these sentences have been underlined.

> <u>Even though I am content at my job</u>, I still keep my eyes open for a new opportunity.

> I always carry an umbrella <u>whenever it looks like rain</u>.

> My aunt, <u>who comes from the Dominican Republic</u>, lives in the Bronx.

A compound sentence is different from a complex sentence because when it is split into two parts, the result is two complete sentences, instead of one complete sentence and a dependent clause.

Compound:
Lois wants to go out to dinner, so Fred met her at the restaurant.

Now we break it down to two complete sentences.

> Lois wants to go out to dinner. Fred met her at the restaurant.

Complex:
Since Lois wants to go out to dinner, Fred met her at the restaurant.

This breaks down to a dependent clause:

> Since Lois wants to go out to dinner

and a complete sentence:

> Fred met her at the restaurant.

When dependent clauses are accidently written as sentences, the result is a sentence fragment.

☞ Practice: Sentence Structure

> **DIRECTIONS:** The following list contains dependent clauses. Add a main clause to each dependent clause to create a complex sentence.

1. although the weather was incredibly hot

2. so that I wouldn't forget them

3. because Leila was nervous

4. when you return from vacation

5. whenever we go to California

6.   who was wearing a white tee shirt

7.   whom you were talking about

8.   that contained our Christmas gifts

9.   that won the contest

10. who was hoping to hear from a friend

Answers

Your answers will be different. Use these suggestions as a guideline.

1.   Although the weather was incredibly hot, Jon worked in the garden.

2.   I left my glasses near my pocketbook, so that I wouldn't forget them.

3.   Because Leila was nervous, she paced up and down the room.

4.   Give me a call when you return from vacation.

5.   Whenever we go to California, we visit our cousins in San Francisco.

6.   The mysterious stranger, who was wearing a white tee shirt, left before I could ask his name.

7.   I know the person whom you were talking about.

8.   Pascal carried the box that contained our Christmas gifts.

9.   This is the photograph that won the contest.

10. Betty, who was hoping to hear from a friend, waited by the telephone.

REVIEW

The ability to vary one's sentence structure is essential for avoiding writing that is dull and repetitive. In the rush to get ideas down, many writers discover that they have used a repetitive sentence structure of subject-verb-prepositional phrase. Once the main points have been written, however, most writers decide to combine sentences in order to make them more varied and interesting. This step is the most pleasurable aspect of writing, for it gives the writer an opportunity to "play" with several versions of the same sentence. By using an independent clause at the beginning of a sentence, the writer can break up a repetitive pattern in a series of sentences. Joining together a string of short sentences with a comma and a conjunction is an excellent way to vary sentence structure. Since there is no one correct way to do this, every writer develops his or her unique method, or style.

The key to varying sentences correctly is to understand how simple sentences become either compound or complex sentences. A compound sentence is when two or more simple sentences are joined together with a comma and a conjunction, while a complex sentence always includes at least one dependent clause that depends on the main clause in order to make sense. Practice varying your simple sentences by turning them into a compound, and then a complex sentence. When you revise a piece of writing, aim for a mixture of simple, compound, and complex sentences. Avoid repeating the same structure throughout.

Spelling and Word Usage

WRITING

SPELLING AND WORD USAGE

SPELLING

At first glance, one would expect *blew* and *sew* to rhyme. Instead, *sew* rhymes with *so*. If words were spelled the way they sound, one would expect *so* to rhyme with *do* instead of *dough* and would never expect *do* to rhyme with *blew.* Confusing, isn't it?

Words are not always spelled phonetically, and it sometimes seems that spelling is totally illogical. However, in spelling there is usually only one correct form.

It is important to learn to spell properly. Poor spelling is usually a sign of haste or carelessness, and it is often taken as a sign of ignorance or illiteracy. Yet learning to spell correctly is indeed more difficult for some people than for others. In any case, it can be mastered with time and patience.

There are many helpful practices to improve spelling: using the dictionary, keeping a list of words that cause difficulty, familiarizing oneself with word origin and the rules in this chapter.

If a writer has absolutely no idea how to spell a word, it obviously cannot be looked up. Yet in most spelling problems, the writer has a general idea of the spelling but is not certain. Even if only the first few letters of the word are known, the writer should be able to find it in the dictionary.

Example:
To check the spelling of the word *miscellaneous.*

The writer probably knows that *misc-* compose the first four letters of the word and might even know a few more by sounding the word out. Although phonetics is not a reliable source for spelling, it can be helpful when using the dictionary. In this particular problem, it most likely is the ending *-aneous* that gives the writer difficulty. Since in the English language there are few words beginning with the letters *misc-,* the writer should have little trouble finding *miscellaneous* in the dictionary.

Example:
To check the spelling of *occasionally.*

Here, the writer is probably concerned with the number of c's and s's. If one looks up the word with the beginning *oca-,* there is no listing. The next logical choice is to check the word with two c's, which will be found a few entries later. One can even skim the page when a general idea of the spelling is known.

When using the dictionary, be sure also that you have found the desired word, not a homonym or a word with a similar form, by checking the word's definition.

Simply enough, checking spelling is a matter of trial and error, so use the dictionary when you are not sure—and even sometimes when you feel certain.

HINTS FOR CORRECT SPELLING

Develop good spelling habits to improve your accuracy.

1. Make certain you know how to pronounce a word correctly. The dictionary listing for each word breaks the word into syllables with a stress mark on the syllable which is accented. This tells you the correct pronunciation of the word.

Example

biography [bi og´ ra phy]

The word biography is pronounced with the accent on the second syllable.

2. Examine the correct word carefully. Try to remember any parts of the spelling that do not seem to make sense phonetically. Memorize them.

3. Practice writing the word after having studied it. If you have misspelled a word, write it ten times. The best way to learn a skill such as spelling is by rote. When a piece of information, such as a spelling word, is repeated often and regularly, it becomes second nature; you do not even have to think about it. Think about why you know certain phone numbers by heart. You have undoubtedly called them so often, or repeated them to so many people that you do not have to stop to think. In the same manner, practicing a list of spelling words you consistently find difficult is the best way to learn them.

4. *Always* proofread your writing carefully to correct misspelled words. Check any word you are uncertain about.

5. Learn the following rule.

I before E, except after C or when sounded like A, as in neighbor and weigh.

Examples

The word is spelled ie following a letter other than C.

thief   field   brief   belief   grief

The word is spelled ei following the letter C.

receive   ceiling   conceited   perceive

These words are exceptions—the ei comes after a letter other than C.)

either   neither   weird   seize   leisure

Another exception is the word *ancient* which is spelled ie, even though it comes after C.

SEDE or CEDE?

Only one word in English ends with the spelling SEDE, the word supersede. All other words which end with the sound "seed" are spelled CEDE or CEED.

Example

precede   concede

succeed   recede

Prefix Spelling Changes

When you add a prefix to a word, do not change the spelling of the original word.

Example

mis + place = misplace

dis + approval = disapproval

mis + spell = misspell

pre + view = preview

un + happy = unhappy

over + anxious = overanxious

dis + satisfaction = dissatisfaction

Suffix Spelling Changes

When you add "ly" or "ness" to a word do not change the spelling of the original word.

careful + ly = carefully

sincere + ly = sincerely

absolute + ly = absolutely

kind + ness = kindness

open + ness = openness

The exception to this rule is for most words that end in "y." For these words, change the "y" to an "i" before adding the "ly" or "ness."

friendly + ness = friendliness

happy + ness = happiness

happy + ly = happily

merry + ly = merrily

Suffixes with Words That End in a Silent "E"

When a suffix begins with a vowel [a, e, i, o, u, and sometimes y] drop the silent "e" from the end of the original word.

reverse + ible = reversible

perverse + ion = perversion

rehearse + al = rehearsal

strange + er = stranger

Suffixes with Words That End in "CE" or "GE"

Keep the silent "e" in the original word before adding a suffix beginning with an "a" or an "o."

advantage + ous = advantageous

change + able = changeable

courage + ous = courageous

Suffixes with Words That End in a Silent "E" and the Suffix Begins with a Consonant

Consonants are all the letters of the alphabet that are NOT vowels. Keep the silent "e" in the original word when adding a suffix that begins with a consonant.

noise + less = noiseless

hope + ful = hopeful

spite + ful = spiteful

state + ment = statement

The exceptions to this rule are

argue + ment = argument

judge + ment = judgment

true + ly = truly

Words Ending in "Y"

When the original word ends in a consonant followed by the letter "y," change the "y" to an "i" as long as the suffix itself does not begin with an "i."

cry + ed = cried

try + ed = tried

lazy + ness = laziness

crazy + ly = crazily

easy + est = easiest

If the suffix itself begins with an "i," then keep the "y" in the original word.

carry + ing = carrying

worry + ing = worrying

stay + ed = stayed

pray + ed = prayed

obey + ed = obeyed

The exception to this rule is when the original word ends in a vowel plus the letter "y."

Double the last letter in a word if it ends in a consonant, before you add the suffixes "ing," "ed," or "est" to a one-syllable word that ends in a single vowel followed by a single consonant.

beg + ing = begging

drug + ist = druggist

hop + ed = hopped

big + est = biggest

quiz + ed = quizzed

The exception to this rule is when words of one syllable end in a consonant preceded by two vowels.

feel + ing = feeling

sleep + ing = sleeping

fair + est = fairest

WORD USAGE

Proper word usage is a skill that is just as important as proper spelling. Sometimes writers will use a word incorrectly so often that they begin to assume that the way they are using it is correct. This is a very bad habit since it makes writing that is actually filled with great ideas seem sloppy and unintelligent. So, practice the drills in this chapter, and practice using the words you find troublesome, as often as you can.

HOMONYMS

Homonyms are words which sound the same, and are sometimes even spelled the same, but have different meanings. When a writer misuses these words, not only has he or she changed the meaning of a sentence, but has given a poor impression of his or her command of the English language. Therefore, it is imperative that you learn these often confusing homonym pairs. Study the section "Words often Confused," and read the sentences given as examples of correct usage. These examples should help you understand when to use each word.

WORDS OFTEN CONFUSED

accept/except

Accept means to agree to something or to receive something.

Except means to leave out.

Cathy <u>accepted</u> Meryl's suggestion.

Everyone <u>except</u> Marty is receiving a raise.

all ready/already

All ready means completely prepared or ready.

Already means something happened previously.

I left the laundry <u>all ready</u> to be folded.

He <u>already</u> warned you about the loose steering.

desert/dessert

Desert means to abandon.

Dessert is served at the end of a meal.

Dennis <u>deserted</u> his family, leaving them miserable.

Because she is watching her weight, she skipped <u>dessert</u>.

hear/here

Hear means to listen.

Here is an adverb referring to this place.

Can you <u>hear</u> me with the radio so loud?

We can stop to rest <u>here</u>.

its/it's

Its is a possessive pronoun.

It's is a contraction for "it is."

The dog wagged <u>its</u> tail.

<u>It's</u> a shame that you missed his performance.

lay/lie

To *lay* means to put down.

To *lie* means to recline.

<u>Lay</u> your groceries down on the counter.

If you feel sick, go <u>lie</u> down.

past/passed

Past refers to something that has already happened.

Passed is the past tense of "to pass." It means something went by.

During the <u>past</u> few summers, I hung around at the beach.

The parade <u>passed</u> before I could see the school's float.

piece/peace

Piece refers to a part of something.

Peace means calm or a lack of fighting.

Have another <u>piece</u> of my chocolate cake.

The troops are trying to maintain <u>peace</u> in Bosnia.

principal/principle

Principal refers to something of importance or to the head of a school.

Principle is an idea generally accepted or understood to be true.

Getting a good job is of <u>principal</u> importance to every graduate.

It is important to understand the <u>principles</u> on which our country is based.

stationary/stationery

Stationary refers to something that doesn't move.

Stationery refers to paper and envelopes for writing letters.

The statue is a <u>stationary</u> figure in the plaza.

We gave our teacher some <u>stationery</u> as a Christmas gift.

there/their/they're

There is an adverb referring to something in a certain place.

Their is a plural possessive pronoun.

They're is a contraction of the words "they are."

When you go <u>there</u>, give them my regards.

<u>Their</u> aunt is coming to visit for a week.

<u>They're</u> leaving for Washington soon.

to/too/two

To is a preposition meaning toward, in the direction of.

Too is an adverb meaning also or very.

Two is a number.

Are you going <u>to</u> the party?

I'd like to come, <u>too</u>.

If you give me <u>two</u> minutes, I'll get ready.

weather/whether

Weather describes the temperature or climate in a given area.

Whether shows a choice.

The <u>weather</u> in Honolulu is always warm.

<u>Whether</u> or not she will travel is uncertain.

whose/who's

Whose is a possessive pronoun.

Who's is a contraction for "who is."

<u>Whose</u> car has its headlights on?

<u>Who's</u> going to tell her that her car battery is dead?

your/you're

Your is a possessive pronoun.

You're is a contraction of the words "you are."

Please give <u>your</u> wife my regards.

<u>You're</u> the kindest person I've ever met.

WORD ANALYSIS

A basic knowledge of the English language, especially familiarity with its numerous prefixes, can help build vocabulary and also strengthen spelling skills. For example, if one knows that *inter-* means *between* and that *intra-* means *within,* one is not likely to spell *intramural* as *intermural*. (The former means within the limits of a city, a college, etc.)

The table shown on the following page lists some common Latin and Greek prefixes, which form part of the foundation of the English language.

Questions

Some of the following words have been misspelled. If you think the word has been spelled correctly, write "C" in the blank space.

1. acheive

2. disatisfied

3. unnusual

PREFIX	MEANING	ENGLISH EXAMPLE
ab-, a-, abs-	away, from	abstain
ad-	to, toward	adjacent
ante-	before	antecedent
anti-	against	antidote
bi-	two	bisect
cata-, cat-, cath-	down	cataclysm
circum-	around	circumlocution
contra-	against	contrary
de-	down, from	decline
di-	twice	diatonic
dis-, di-	apart, away	dissolve
epi-, ep-, eph-	upon, among	epidemic
ex-, e-	out of, from	extricate
hyper-	beyond, over	hyperactive
hypo-	under, down, less	hypodermic
in-	in, into	instill
inter-	among, between	intercede
intra-	within	intramural
meta-, met-	beyond, along with	metaphysics
mono-	one	monolith
non-	no, not	nonsense
ob-	against	obstruct
para-, par-	beside	parallel
per-	through	permeate
pre-	before	prehistoric
pro-	before	project
super-	above	superior
tele-, tel-	far	television
trans-	across	transpose
ultra-	beyond	ultraviolet

4. misspelled

5. easyily

6. prosede

7. couragous

8. recieve

9. retreaval

10. closeing

11. puppys

12. choped

13. hopeful

14. arguement

15. steadyly

16. sleepping

17. reverseible

18. tomatos

19. quized

20. truely

Answers

1. achieve (I before E, except after C)

2. dissatisfied (When adding a prefix, do not change the spelling of the original word.)

3. unusual (When adding a prefix, do not change the spelling of the original word.)

4. misspelled is correctly spelled. (When

adding a prefix, do not change the spelling of the original word.)

5. easily (When a word ends in "y," change the "y" to an "i" before adding the "ly.")

6. proceed (All words other than "super-cede" which end with the sound "seed" are spelled "cede" or "ceed.")

7. courageous (When a word ends in "ge," keep the "e" before adding the suffix "ous.")

8. receive (I before E, except after C)

9. retrieval (I before E, except after C)

10. closing (When a suffix begins with a vowel, drop the silent "e" from the end of the original word before adding the suffix.)

11. puppies (Review spelling of plural nouns.)

12. chopped (Double the last letter in a word if it ends in a consonant before you add the suffix "ed" to a one-syllable word that ends in a single vowel followed by a single consonant.)

13. hopeful is correctly spelled. (Keep the silent "e" in the original word when adding a suffix that begins with a consonant.)

14. argument (This word is an exception to the rule which requires keeping the silent "e" in the original word when adding a suffix that begins with a consonant.)

15. steadily (When the original word ends in a consonant followed by "y," the "y" is changed to an "i" before adding the suffix.)

16. sleeping (When words of one syllable end in a consonant preceded by two vowels, do not double the last consonant in the original word.)

17. reversible (When a suffix begins with a

vowel, drop the silent "e" from the end of the original word.)

18. tomatoes (Review spelling of plural nouns.)

19. quizzed (Double the last letter in a word if it ends in a consonant before adding the suffix "ed" to a one-syllable word that ends in a single vowel followed by a single consonant.)

20. truly (This is an exception to the rule about keeping the silent "e" in the original word when adding a suffix that begins with a consonant.)

Homonyms are words which are often confused. The following sentences have homonyms in parentheses. Circle the word you believe is used correctly in the sentence.

Questions

1. Mary was so (board, bored) with the lecture that she almost fell asleep.

2. Washington, D.C. is the (capitol, capital) of the United States.

3. The cement felt (coarse, course) against his (bear, bare) feet.

4. You should (council, counsel) Harry on his inappropriate behavior.

5. I had (two, too) ice cream (sundaes, sundays) for (desert, dessert) after lunch and now I can't eat a thing for dinner.

6. Ruby will graduate (fourth, forth) in her class.

7. You (great, grate) the cheese and I'll slice the tomatoes.

8. I would like to learn how to ride a (horse, hoarse).

9. The cat fed (it's, its) kittens.

10. The bride wanted to (where, wear) something old and something (knew, new).

11. Was there ever a time when (there, their) was (piece, peace) in the world?

12. I saw a good (sale, sail) on a (pear, pair) of shoes.

13. Someday, I will become a pilot of a (plane, plain).

14. Please put some more mustard on that hotdog (roll, role).

15. The (site, sight) of the conference was in a great location near the beach.

16. The (soul, sole) of my sneaker is wearing away.

17. (Where, Wear) will you be tonight?

18. That interview was really a (waist, waste) of time.

19. That virus made me feel so (weak, week).

20. (Whether, Weather) or not he wants to pursue his career for a lifetime is up to him.

21. I would like to (weigh, way) myself on the scale but I am afraid I did not lose any pounds.

22. (Here, Hear) today, gone tomorrow.

23. (Which, Witch) way did he go, George?

24. There's a (hole, whole) in the bucket.

25. (Who's, Whose) turn is it anyway?

Answers

1. bored. **Bored** is the correct answer. **Bored** means not interested. **Board** means a piece of wood.

2. capital. **Capital** is the correct answer. **Capital** means a city were government meets. **Capitol** means a building where a governmental body meets.

3. coarse, bare. **Coarse** is the correct answer. **Coarse** means rough. **Course** means a subject studied in school. **Bare** is the correct answer. **Bare** means not wearing any clothes. **Bear** refers to an animal.

4. counsel. **Counsel** is the correct answer. **Counsel** means to advise someone. **Council** means a governing group, like a city council that governs a city.

5. two, sundaes, dessert, dinner. **Two** is the correct answer. **Two** means the number two. **Too** is an adverb meaning also or very. **Sundaes** is the correct answer. A **sundae** is made up of ice cream, whipped cream, chocolate or strawberry syrup, and has a cherry on top. **Sunday** is a day of the week. **Dessert** is the correct answer. **Dessert** is served at the end of a meal. **Desert** means to abandon.

6. fourth. **Fourth** is the correct answer. **Fourth** is a number. **Forth** means going forward.

7. grate. **Grate** is the correct answer. **Grate** means to grind. **Great** means being well known, like a celebrity.

8. horse. **Horse** is the correct answer. **Horse** is a type of an animal. **Hoarse** means having a rough, husky voice.

9. its. **Its** is the correct answer. **Its** is a possessive pronoun. **It's** is a contraction for the words "it is."

10. wear, new. **Wear** is the correct answer. **Wear** refers to clothing. **Where** refers to a place. **New** is the correct answer. **New** means a recent purchase. **Knew** is the past tense of "to know."

11. there, peace. **There** is the correct answer. **There** is an adverb referring to something in a certain place. **Their** is a possessive pronoun. **Peace** is the correct answer. **Peace** means calm or lack of fighting. **Piece** means a part of something.

12. sale, pair. **Sale** is the correct answer. **Sale** means buying an item at a reduced price. **Sail** means a part of a boat that directs its course. **Pair** is the correct answer. **Pair** refers to two items that are the same. **Pear** is a fruit.

13. plane. **Plane** is the correct answer. **Plane** is an airplane. **Plain** means not fancy.

14. roll. **Roll** is the correct answer. **Roll** is a type of bread served at a meal. **Role** means a part in a play.

15. site. **Site** is the correct answer. **Site** means location. **Sight** means vision.

16. sole. **Sole** is the correct answer. **Sole** means the underside of a shoe. **Soul** is the inner being of a person.

17. where. **Where** is the correct answer. **Where** refers to a place. **Wear** refers to clothing.

18. waste. **Waste** is the correct answer. **Waste** means not having a use. **Waist** is the middle portion of the body.

19. weak. **Weak** is the correct answer. **Weak** means lacking strength. **Week** means a period of time: seven days.

20. whether. **Whether** is the correct answer. **Whether** shows a choice. **Weather** describes temperature or climate in a particular area.

21. weigh, lose. **Weigh** is the correct answer. **Weigh** refers to the heaviness of a person or object. **Way** is a course of action.

22. here. **Here** is the correct answer. **Here** refers to a place. **Hear** means listen.

23. which. **Which** is the correct answer. **Which** refers to a direction. A **witch** is a woman who has magical powers and casts spells.

24. hole. **Hole** is the correct answer. **Hole** is an opening. **Whole** means complete.

25. whose. **Whose** is the correct answer. **Whose** is a possessive pronoun. **Who's** is a contraction for who is.

☞ Practice: Spelling and Word Usage

DIRECTIONS: The following sentences have a pair of words often confused in parentheses. Circle the word you believe is used correctly in the sentence.

1. My parents will be (here, hear) at noon.

2. The (principle, principal) of Central High School will retire in June.

3. (You're, Your) going to need to buy warm clothing if you plan to go on a cruise to Alaska.

4. My supervisor (excepted, accepted) my letter of resignation.

5. My mother-in-law plans to bake an angel food cake for (desert, dessert).

6. According to the (weather, whether) report, (it's, its) going to rain every day this week.

7. For the (passed, past) year, I have been enrolled in the GED program at Midland Community College.

8. Please cut me a (peace, piece) of pecan pie.

9. (There, Their, They're) are planning to sell (there, their, they're) home and move to Florida.

10. (Two, To, Too) students were selected (two, to, too) the hospitality committee from the freshman class.

Answers

1. here. **Here** is the correct answer. **Here** is an adverb referring to a place. **Hear** means to listen.

2. principal. **Principal** is the correct answer. **Principal** refers to the head of a school. **Principle** refers to an idea that is accepted as truth.

3. You're. **You're** is the correct answer. **You're** is a contraction for the words "you are." **Your** is a possessive pronoun.

4. accepted. **Accept** means to agree or to receive something. **Except** means to leave out.

5. dessert. **Dessert** is the correct answer. **Dessert** is served at the end of a meal. **Desert** means to abandon.

6. weather, it's. **Weather** is the correct answer. **Weather** describes temperature or climate in a particular area. **Whether** shows a choice. **It's** is the correct answer. **It's** is the contraction for the words "it is." **Its** is a possessive pronoun.

7. past. **Past** is the correct answer. **Past** refers to something that has already happened. **Passed** is the past tense of "to pass."

8. piece. **Piece** is the correct answer. **Piece** refers to a part of something. **Peace** means calm or lack of fighting.

9. They're, their. **They're** is the correct answer. **They're** is a contraction for the words "they are." **Their** is the correct answer. **Their** is a possessive pronoun. **There** is an adverb referring to something in a certain place.

10. Two, to. **Two** is the correct answer. **Two** is a number. **To** is the correct answer. **To** is a preposition meaning toward, in the direction of. **Too** is an adverb meaning also or very.

REVIEW

Undoubtedly, mastering the rules of spelling and word usage is one of the more difficult skills taught in this book. The difficulty lies not in the logic behind the concept, but in the many variations and exceptions to the spelling rules. Homonyms are especially tricky.

While studying the rules is a good idea for developing an idea of the logic behind writing in English, the best way to be consistently correct is to practice, practice, practice! Just as school children take spelling tests in order to memorize correct spelling, so should you give yourself spelling tests of the words you consistently spell incorrectly. Writing and rewriting the word is preferable to merely looking at its correct spelling. The repetitive act of writing helps "etch" the correct spelling into the brain.

In our age of computer writing programs complete with "spell checks," not to mention the abundance of hand-held dictionaries, many people question the point in learning to spell at all. While it is true that it is easier than ever to check one's spelling, there is no substitute for knowing how to spell. Developing an understanding of the English language is far preferable to using a computer; after all, the computer is a machine, a sophisticated one to be sure, but a machine that relies on humans to program it!

Being correct in your spelling and usage will afford you the confidence that will serve you well when you take an exam in college, or interview for a job. College professors and employers alike are put off by working with people whose grasp of the English language is weak. No matter how intelligent or hard-working you may be, the higher grade or the better position will go to an equally intelligent or hard-working person who can communicate clearly and correctly. So dedicate yourself to learning the rules in this chapter, and you will be pleased with the success it brings.

Steps in the Writing Process

WRITING

STEPS IN THE WRITING PROCESS

INTRODUCTION TO WRITING

Journals

The best way for you to prepare to take the GED writing exam is to become as comfortable as possible with writing. Few things cause as much panic in otherwise confident adults as being asked to write an essay! Many people are intimidated by the thought of having to fill all that blank space and find they have "nothing to say." Even worse, many people are worried about making grammatical mistakes or not knowing how to use punctuation correctly. Strange as it may sound, the best way to overcome your fear of writing is to write as often as possible. A journal is the best way to accomplish this; since it is entirely private (unless you choose to share it with someone), you need not worry about making mistakes. You can concentrate on expressing your thoughts instead of being "correct."

Discipline yourself to write in your journal every day. Find a time that is convenient for you and stick to it. Buy yourself a notebook or steno pad and bring it with you to work (during lunch hours or while commuting might be ideal times to spend writing for ten or fifteen minutes), or leave it at your bedside so you can write before you go to sleep. The important thing is to write in it regularly.

What should you write about? Whatever stray thoughts are in your head make an excellent starting point. Just write down random words or ideas. Do not worry about sentences, spelling, or grammar just yet. As you write an idea that may have been stuck in your mind all day, you will be surprised at how easily other thoughts begin to tumble onto the page.

Here is a sample from one woman's journal:

> The traffic today was terrible! So frustrating, sitting there and not being able to do anything! My head is pounding from having to concentrate on driving and there was nothing I wanted to hear on the radio! I must spend half my life commuting to work. I wonder what it's like living in a small town? No traffic jams, maybe less pressure? Sounds perfect, but then why do people in small towns want to move to the city? Still, it might be worth looking into. Maybe next weekend, I'll look around in Rocky Hill. Look in the newspaper, see what kind of jobs are available out there. Anyway, it will make a nice weekend getaway.

Notice how this writer's frustration with a traffic jam led her to think of alternatives to her current lifestyle. Not only has she come up with some new ideas, but by letting her thoughts go, she has come up with several possible topics to write about. What possible essay topics could be found within this journal free-writing example? How about an essay on the contrast between small town and big city life? The writer certainly came up with some ideas on that topic. In fact, nearly any of her sentences could be developed into complete paragraphs. Later on, we will discuss how to turn a journal entry into an essay.

If you have trouble getting started, you can try a technique called free-writing. Free-writing is rather like word association: you write down a word which in turn reminds you of another word or phrase, and so on. To get a feeling for how free-writing works, take a look at the example below.

Example:
The word *snow* brings to mind many images. When one student wrote them down, he came up with these words: *icy, crystal-like, pure, shoveling, hot cocoa, warm, kitchen.*

Try it yourself with the following words:

marriage

prejudice

responsibility

money

Now try free-writing sentences. Start with any of the incomplete sentences below or make up some of your own. Finish the sentence with whatever comes to mind. If you discover that you have more to say, great! Keep going with the idea you have.

I really dislike my boss because . . .

This room reminds me of . . .

I worry most about . . .

More than anything, I want . . .

It's not fair that . . .

Example:
I really dislike my boss because she has a habit of making me feel stupid. I think I understand what she's telling me to do, but when I show her what I've done, she rolls her eyes and tells me in this overly patient voice, "No, this isn't what I said.

Why don't we try again?" What does she mean "we"? I'm the one sitting there at my desk, nervous and upset because I'm really not sure what she wants! I think the problem is hers! If she would just tell me what she wants, I could do it, but I'm not a mind reader!

Free-writing works because it loosens up your mind and enables you to get something down on paper. Once you have actually written something, it can be improved, whereas if you haven't written anything, there is no way to make it better. Finding a topic to write about, or finding more to say about a topic is what most people find intimidating. Use free-writing even if you have a topic, but are having trouble thinking of how to develop it into a journal entry.

Let's say you already have a topic. You want to write about whether or not governments have the right to ban smoking in public places. How can free-writing help you develop this topic? Whether or not you already have an opinion on this topic, make a list of all the reasons you think smoking should legally be banned. Then make a list of reasons why smokers should have a right to smoke in public. For each item on the list, begin to write whatever comes to mind. If one of the items on your list was that people can get sick from inhaling second-hand smoke, you might write the following:

People can get sick from inhaling second-hand smoke. This is so unfair, it really gets me mad! Why should an innocent person get sick when he himself wasn't doing anything wrong? If anyone wants to smoke, knowing it could harm them, then that's their business but it shouldn't be legal to do something in a public place that could have a negative effect on other people.

Continue free-writing until you have come

up with something to say for each of the ideas you have listed. You will be pleased with some of what you have written; some may not yield anything worth developing further. You can always eliminate what doesn't work, or you can come back to it later to see if a fresh approach will produce better results.

As you look back at some of your journal entries, select one or two for revision. Using the techniques you have learned in this book, see if you can reword some of the sentences to make them clearer. See if the exercises you have been doing have sharpened your awareness of grammar and usage. The freewriting passage above contains some weak sentences, run-ons, and other errors. Using it as a model, see if you can improve on it.

Whatever revisions you decide to make will not only improve your writing, but are excellent practice for writing the GED essay segment.

THE WRITING PROCESS

When you write in your journal, no one sees what you have written except for you. No one will judge the quality of what you have written. While journals are an extremely useful way to become comfortable with expressing yourself in written form, there are many times when you will need to write in order to communicate to others. When you are writing in order to communicate, you must be clear, coherent, and logical; otherwise, you run the risk of being misread.

Nobody, not even professional writers, can sit down at a desk, get an idea, and begin to write. All writers follow a process which begins with getting an idea, organizing it, developing it, and perfecting it as a final product. By breaking a writing task down into manageable stages, you will be able to express your ideas much more effectively.

The process most writers use breaks down into roughly four parts: prewriting, writing a rough draft, organizing and revising, and proofreading.

Using this process does not mean that you will have to write four drafts! You should write one rough draft, double-spaced. Then, as you re-read what you have written, write any changes or revisions in between the lines. Some people find it helpful to write "Insert A" or "Insert B" over the space where they want to include more than a few words. Then, they write the long insert on a separate piece of paper marked "A" or "B." Continue re-reading your essay until you are pleased with it. Then neatly copy over the finished product. Proofread it at least twice to make certain you have not left anything out or written a word twice.

PREWRITING

Sometimes you are asked to write an essay on a specific topic, while at other times you are given free reign as to what to write. In either case, most people have a difficult time deciding how to fill all that blank space. By using the free-writing techniques described in the "Journal" section, you can learn how to generate ideas for your essay.

Determining Your Purpose

Read the essay question and decide on what the purpose of the essay will be. Will it be to persuade your reader? Or do you need to explain something? Suppose the question reads as follows:

> "Television is bad for people. Do you agree or disagree with this statement?"

Make your decision and be very clear about how you feel. Don't be wishy-washy; take a firm stand. Here are two possible ways to begin which clearly and strongly state an opinion, depending on your point of view:

> "I agree that television is bad for people."

> "Since television is an excellent learning tool, it is good for people."

Gathering Ideas

Now that you have made your stand, you need to prove what you are saying. The way to do this is by offering evidence in the form of details and examples. Jot down a few phrases that show ideas or examples which support your point of view. Do this quickly on a separate sheet of paper, spending no more than five minutes on the task. You might try jotting your ideas down in a "cluster web." A cluster web is a diagram of one idea literally leading to another.

Outlining Your Rough Draft

Making an outline is the next logical step in preparing a paper. It requires only a short time to prepare, and it helps tremendously when actually writing the paper. An outline is a plan, guiding you through the paper in clear and logical steps.

When writing the outline, you should take all the best ideas from your prewriting list or cluster web. Arrange these ideas in order of importance. You might decide to begin with the most important idea and work your way down your list to the least important, or you can begin with the least important idea and build up to the most important, ending on that point.

Group all similar ideas under a main idea and give that main idea a title. Each main idea is numbered with a Roman numeral. Under each Roman numeral, list the similar, supporting ideas in ABC order, as done in the sample outline shown here.

Reasons Television Is Bad — (topic)

I. Television takes time away from other things — *(main idea)*

A. more productive things could be done — *(supporting idea)*

B. could be outside, enjoying nature — *(supporting idea)*

C. people use TV to avoid unpleasant tasks — *(supporting idea)*

II. Programs are often of poor quality — *(main idea)*

A. many TV shows are basically silly sitcoms — *(supporting idea)*

B. depict crimes that people later copy — *(supporting idea)*

C. unrealistic — *(supporting idea)*

III. Television can become addictive — *(main idea)*

A. schedules get arranged based on when a show is playing — *(supporting idea)*

B. TV is watched instead of socializing — *(supporting idea)*

This outline gives you an overview of what your essay will look like. Based on this outline, the essay on why television is bad will contain three paragraphs of supportive evidence and details, plus the introductory and concluding paragraphs.

WRITING A ROUGH DRAFT

Spend about 20 minutes writing your rough draft. It should consist of approximately five paragraphs: the introduction, three paragraphs of supportive evidence, and the conclusion.

The Introduction

Begin with your thesis statement, which is a sentence that tells the general point of view of your essay. A good thesis statement should basically summarize your main idea. The the-

sis "controls" your essay. By this we mean that you should continually refer to your thesis statement as you write the essay to make certain you have stayed with the main idea.

Do not repeat the question you are answering. This sometimes produces an awkward sentence. Review your outline and develop a sentence that states your purpose in writing. Examine these possible thesis statements:

I agree with the statement that television is bad for people.

Television is not the best.

Of all the pastimes available to modern people, television is the biggest waste of time.

The first sentence merely restates the question, while the second sentence is unclear. The third sentence, however, is a good thesis statement since it summarizes all the points listed in the outline, clearly and interestingly.

Next, continue developing the introduction by writing a few sentences explaining what you mean and generally stating the ideas which will support your thesis.

Questions

Choose the best thesis statement for both topics.

Topic A: Capital punishment as a deterrent to crime.

1. I don't believe in capital punishment.

2. Capital punishment isn't fair or foolproof.

3. As history proves, capital punishment is rarely a deterrent to crime.

Topic B: What is the best time to start a family?

1. The best time to begin a family; it depends.

2. The best time to begin a family is when you are emotionally ready to make an enormous commitment of time, money, and love.

3. There is no best time to begin a family.

Answers

Topic A

Sentence #3. Sentence #1 merely announces your position, while sentence #2 is vague. Sentence #3 clearly indicates that the writer will use historical data to prove that capital punishment is not a deterrent to crime.

Topic B

Sentence #2. Sentence #1 is vague. It offers no idea of what the decision is dependent on. Sentence #3 simply restates the topic. Sentence #2 summarizes what will later be developed in the body of the essay.

The Body

The body of your rough draft will consist of at least three paragraphs of supportive evidence. Each of your three main ideas from the introduction should now be developed fully into its own paragraph. It is essential that you develop your paragraph by supporting your ideas with good examples. The following paragraph is an example of unsupported writing.

Example:
Watching television takes time away from other things. Programs on television are often stupid and depict crimes that people later copy. Television takes time away from loved ones. And it then becomes addictive. So, television is bad for people because it is no good.

In this example, the writer has not given any concrete evidence for any of the good ideas

mentioned. He or she assumes the reader will see the point and agree. However, any one of the sentences within the paragraph could make a good opening sentence for a whole paragraph of supportive evidence. Notice how the following paragraph results from the sentence of the first paragraph.

Example:
Watching television takes time away from other things. For example, all those hours people spend sitting in front of the television could be spent working on building a shelf or fixing the roof. Maybe the laundry needs to be done, but because people watch television, they may have no time to do it. Someone could be out enjoying a beautiful day in the park, but miss the opportunity because he or she just had to stay home to catch a favorite soap opera on the TV. Watching television definitely keeps people from getting things done.

Continue to develop the essay by following your outline and writing additional paragraphs which give support and development to your ideas.

You can find the details you need by doing any of the following:

- give facts to prove your ideas
- use an example to illustrate what you are talking about
- tell a brief story to enhance your point
- define a term which your reader may not fully understand

This example uses a fact to develop the topic sentence about secondhand smoke.

Secondhand smoke is dangerous. The American Medical Association published a recent study showing that 35% of all lung cancers were caused by secondhand smoke.

Using specific examples is another good way to develop a topic sentence.

> Watching television takes time away from other things. Instead of watching television, people could fly a kite or plant a garden. Watching television takes time away from doing housework and from spending time with children.

Telling a brief story is a great method for developing a topic sentence into a paragraph, as long as the story is short and appropriate to the essay.

> Sailing without prior experience can be hazardous! I once pretended to know more about sailing than I actually did, just so I could go with my boyfriend on his boss' boat. Even though I had never sailed before, I foolishly didn't tell anybody. As a result, I let go of the spinnaker sail too quickly, and ended up dumping everyone — the boss included — into the water.

Sometimes, defining an uncommon term can best develop your topic sentence.

> If you like spicy foods, try Szechuan cuisine. This type of Chinese cooking originated in the Szechuan province of China, where very hot chili peppers are commonly used as an antidote to the intense heat and humidity. The peppers cause you to sweat; therefore, you drink more and stay hydrated in the hot weather.

Each of the following topic sentences has been developed with different types of details. Tell whether each detail is a fact, example, story, or definition.

Questions

Topic A: If you want to appreciate Shakespeare's poetry, read his sonnets.

1. He wrote over 100 sonnets.

2. A sonnet is a poem consisting of 14 lines.

3. "Shall I Compare Thee to a Summer's Day?" is one of my favorite Shakespearean sonnets.

Topic B: Operating a computer involves learning an entirely new language.

1. A mouse, for instance, in computer-speak is not a rodent.

2. I spent hours trying to figure out some of the terms my children use so freely. Finally, they took pity on me and helped me out.

3. There are over 200 computer-related terms in common use today.

Answers

Topic A		Topic B	
1.	fact	1.	example
2.	definition	2.	story
3.	example	3.	fact

The Conclusion

There are several ways to write a concluding paragraph.

One way is to sum up what you have explained in earlier paragraphs and add one final thought.

Example:
So, we can see that television takes away from the quality of life and is therefore bad for human beings. We should be watching the sky, the birds, and each other instead of television.

Another way is to offer a prediction of the future.

Example:

The negative aspects of watching television, as we have seen, are many. Unless people make a point of finding other ways to spend leisure time, the future for the human race is grim. We will have become the most unproductive and antisocial biological creatures on earth.

Many well-written conclusions end with a recommendation.

Example:

In conclusion, it seems that watching television in excess can be detrimental. I recommend that the next time someone in your family sits down to watch television, you offer an enjoyable alternative. Take a walk, cook a meal together, listen to music, or, most importantly, talk to each other.

ORGANIZING AND REVISING THE ROUGH DRAFT

After you have developed the ideas on your prewriting list into about five paragraphs, you should spend approximately ten minutes organizing and editing the rough draft. The main thing you are looking for is to see if your main idea, or thesis, has been demonstrated through examples within unified paragraphs.

The concept of the unified paragraph is a very important one. Basically, a paragraph should contain only one idea which has been explained fully enough for a reader to understand it. If you have written a paragraph which contains several ideas, you need to do some re-organizing. Re-read each paragraph carefully. Ask yourself if what you have said in the last sentence of the paragraph relates back to the first sentence. If the ideas do not relate, then look for the place where you feel you switched topics and make a little proofreader mark [¶] to indicate that you think a new paragraph should begin at that point. Keep reading until

you are satisfied that every paragraph you have written is unified and explains your idea fully.

To help connect one paragraph to the next, as well as to help your ideas flow logically, one to the next, use transitions. Transitions are words or groups of words which link together ideas which are similar, as well as ideas which contradict each other. In order to show a relationship in time or position, use the appropriate transitional word. Cause-and-effect relationships, as well as summaries, are indicated by the use of transitions.

The following chart will provide a handy reference when you need a transitional word or phrase.

To show an example or to summarize

as a result	in any event
in short	in brief
on the whole	in conclusion
for instance	in fact
to sum up	in other words
for example	in any case

To demonstrate a cause/effect relationship or to show a result

as	so
for	because
therefore	since
thus	then
consequently	for this reason
as a result	

To link dissimilar or contradictory ideas

although	otherwise
in spite of	however

as if	provided that
instead	nevertheless
still	but
yet	conversely
on the other hand	on the contrary

To link ideas which are similar

again	for example
likewise	also
for instance	moreover
and further	another
nor	of course
furthermore	in like manner
besides	too
similarly	in addition

Now that your ideas are organized into well-developed, unified paragraphs which flow logically from one to the other, you need to make sure you have the appropriate tone for your essay. When you are writing informally, it is acceptable to use terms such as *I think* or *I believe*. In an informal situation, it is okay to refer to your reader as *you*. However, when you are writing a more formal piece, it is more appropriate to focus on the idea itself, and not on what "you or I" think or believe. Compare the two examples below:

Informal:
If you want to improve your chances for a better job, you should take the GED exam.

Formal:
People who want to improve their chances for a better job should take the GED exam.

As you re-read your essay, decide if the tone is appropriate for your audience. Regardless of whether you intend your tone to be formal or not, make sure you have been consistent. Don't switch in the middle. If you are writing a formal essay, make sure you have not addressed your reader as *you* anywhere within the essay. Experiment with revising your sentences until you have eliminated any informal references.

PROOFREADING

When you proofread, you are looking for errors in spelling, grammar, mechanics, and sentence structure. Spending about five to ten minutes, ask yourself the following questions:

- Are all your sentences really sentences, or have you written some fragments or run-on sentences?

- Is your language appropriate for your audience?

- Is your punctuation correct? Did you capitalize correctly? Did you check for commas, periods, and quotation marks? Have you misspelled any words?

- Is the subject and verb agreement correct in your sentences? Do all your sentences have parallel structure?

- Are any of your modifiers misplaced?

- Have you misused any words?

One good technique you can use to discover errors is called "voicing." Voicing involves reading aloud what you have written. It may sound strange, but often your eye will skip over an error that your ear will pick up. Therefore, as you read aloud, you may hear a mistake that you will not notice, regardless of how many times you re-read it. If you are in a test-taking situation and cannot read aloud, try just moving your lips as you read silently. You will be surprised at how many errors you can catch by using this method.

Questions

Each of the following sentences is incorrect. Determine what is wrong with each of them and make the necessary corrections.

1. rather than go shopping at the mall.

2. I liked the movie "Jerry Maguire" and I really recommend it because it was so enjoyable.

3. Your point it stinks and I think that people who share your opinion are really stupid.

4. Waiting for the subway, the off-duty patrolman found a wallet on the ground.

5. I enjoyed computer classes and to study the travel business.

6. I discovered the music of Dave Matthews and Tom Petty which was terrific at my party.

7. We cannot make deliveries of furniture over 20 yards.

8. We could of left earlier, but having a house full of kids make us late every time.

9. We admire Professor Godwinn however we prefer taking classes with Dr. Nash.

10. In the long run, the most important thing is not to be effected by the affects of our country's political situation.

Answers

The errors have been identified and explained for you. However, since there is often more than one way to correct many of these sentences, the following answers are guidelines.

1. This group of words is a fragment, not a sentence, since it has no subject or verb to complete it

    I was hoping to jog along the ocean rather than go shopping at the mall.

2. This is a run on sentence. It is missing punctuation.

    I liked the movie "Jerry Maguire." I really recommend it because it was so enjoyable.

3. This sentence contains inappropriate language.

    I seriously disagree with your point, and I believe the people who share your opinion need to consider the broader picture.

4. This sentence contains a misplaced modifier.

    While waiting for the subway, the off-duty patrolman found a wallet on the ground.

5. This sentence lacks parallel structure.

    I enjoyed taking computer classes and studying the travel business.

6. This sentence is confusing because the reader cannot be sure to which musician the word "which" refers: Dave Matthews or Tom Petty, or both.

    I discovered the music of Dave Matthews and Tom Petty both of which were terrific at my party.

7. This sentence is confusing because it is not clear what the 20 yards refers to. Does it refer to the length of the furniture or the distance the furniture is to be delivered?

8. This sentence contains two major errors. The phrase "could of" should have been "could have," since "of" is never part of the verb.

Also, the verb "make" does not agree with the subject "house."

> We could have left earlier, but having a house full of kids makes us late every time.

9.   This sentence is a run on because it lacks punctuation.

> We admire Professor Godwinn, however we prefer taking classes with Dr. Nash.

10.   The words "effect" and "affect" have been misused in both instances.

> In the long run, the most important thing is not to be affected by the effects of our country's political situation.

☞ Practice: Writing an Essay

> **DIRECTIONS**: Give yourself 45 minutes to write an essay on the topic below. Make sure to time yourself. Write only on the topic provided. Remember to use the strategies which you learned in this chapter.

Americans are, as a nation, vastly overweight and under exercised. Despite the fact that we have access to everything needed to maintain a healthy lifestyle, Americans continue to eat excessively and unhealthily.

Do you agree or disagree with this statement? Respond to this in an essay of approximately 200 words, making sure to support your view with examples using your own past experiences or knowledge of other people's experiences.

The following three essays are samples of essays written in response to the question you just answered. Each essay has been analyzed so that you can clearly identify its strengths and weaknesses.

Essay One

During the last half of the twentieth century, the American public has been bombarded with the news that we are overfed and lazy. Hardly a day goes by without some new study trumpeting the latest data proving that our diet is unhealthy and a leading cause of many diseases. Although we are the richest nation in the world, our diet has been compared unfavorably to that of third world nations. Endless editorials bemoan the "coach potato" existence of our citizens who, it seems, would rather flip through the television channels endlessly than get physical exercise. Assuming that the bad press we Americans receive is accurate, how seriously should we consider a change? My belief is that we should stop worrying so much and learn to enjoy life, even if it means a life with a few extra pounds.

Of course, I am not talking about the seriously obese, or others with life threatening conditions caused by overweight or otherwise unhealthy eating habits. Instead, I believe that our national obsession with dieting and living up to the standard of unrealistically thin models is foolish, and has probably contributed more than anything else to our collective overweight. After all, models are underweight for professional reasons. Furthermore, they are able to become models because their body types are naturally thin. This is not true, however, for the majority of us. A person of normal weight looks heavy when compared to a rail thin fashion model. Since attaining the "look" with which we are confronted daily in magazines and movies is difficult, if not impossible to attain, is it any wonder that most people feel hopeless, and resort to overeating out of frustration?

If sanity would prevail in our thinking, all these reports of "errors in eating" would stop. Instead of obsessing about our diets and exercise programs, scientists and nutritionists should suggest a diet of moderation. Let's forget about counting calories and grams of fat, and weighing portions of food. If we would just eat when we were hungry and ate only until we were pleasantly full, and if our meals consisted of foods we enjoy, we would not get fat. Additionally, if we walked or rode bicycles more often, instead of taking the car or the bus everywhere, we would not need to join expensive health clubs or buy exercise equipment which winds up unused, anyway. Meanwhile, despite the news of our national overweight, we are simultaneously confronted with a serious epidemic of eating disorders among adolescents, girls in particular. Several of my friends who are teachers have reported that it is not uncommon for girls as young as eight or nine to avoid eating breakfast or skip lunch in hope of losing weight. Nearly half my friends' high school students are on diets, and worst of all, most of them are girls of normal weight who view themselves as being fat.

Although it may seem unfashionable to advocate ending our fixation with diet and exercise, I think it is time we learned to relax and accept a few extra pounds. After all, I once read in the newspaper that the difference in life expectancy for an overweight person and a person whose weight is considered "normal" is only four months! I truly believe that our lives would be more pleasurable, if indeed four months shorter, if we learned to accept moderation as the only diet advice necessary for good health.

Analysis of Essay One

This essay scores between 6 and 5. The writer has stuck to the assigned topic, and has made no errors in grammar, mechanics, or usage. The essay contains varied sentence structure, transitions which help direct the flow of ideas, well-balanced paragraphs, and sufficient examples to support the writer's thesis.

The first paragraph leads up to the writer's

thesis statement, which appears as the last sentence of the paragraph. The thesis, "that we should stop worrying so much and learn to enjoy life…" clearly disagrees with the statement in the question.

The topic sentence in the second paragraph is its second sentence, "Instead, I believe that our national obsession with dieting and living up to the standard of unrealistically thin models is foolish, and has probably contributed more than anything else to our collective overweight." This topic is supported by using obvious, widely known facts.

In the third paragraph, the writer makes a recommendation to advocate "a diet of moderation," and supports this topic by using anecdotal evidence gathered from friends, as suggested in the essay question.

The conclusion restates the thesis and provides an additional piece of factual information regarding the slight difference in life expectancy between overweight and normal weight people. This leads naturally into the writer's prediction that life would be more enjoyable if we practiced moderation rather than obsess about our diets.

Essay Two

I agree with the statement that the majority of Americans are overweight and do not exercise enough. While there are people who diet and exercise, there are an awful lot of people who don't. It is true that Americans have access to everything they need to maintain a healthy lifestyle. I think that people who are interested in a healthy lifestyle read articles about diet and exercise, and people who are not interested don't. This explains why most people are overweight. This just means that there is no connection necessarily between availability of information and actually living a healthy lifestyle.

For instance, I read a lot of magazine articles about fitness, but to tell you the truth, I'm a little overweight. This proves that even though I have everything with regard to the information I need to maintain a healthy lifestyle, I don't necessarily follow it. If this is true for me, it must be true for many others as well. There is plenty of information around giving government guidelines about healthy eating. There are diet articles every month in magazines. There are health clubs all over town and if you listen to news reports, everyone is out jogging. So why are so many of us overweight?

Being overweight is dangerous and unattractive. Not exercising enough keeps you from feeling full of energy. I saw somewhere that the U.S. government came out with a recommendation that we should eat very little fat, a limited amount of dairy products, and a large amount of grains, fruits, and vegetables. This is good diet advice, but I know a lot of people who think that every meal should include a big hunk of steak or chicken, and who put butter on everything. The government as well as many doctors recommend that we all exercise at least three times a week, but most Americans get their exercise by flipping through channels on the TV remote control. We'd all be healthier if we listened to the recommendations we've been getting!

In conclusion, there is a lot of information available to us about how to stay healthy, but we don't pay enough attention to it. That is why it is true that most Americans are overweight and under exercised.

Analysis of Essay Two

This essay scores between a 4 and 3. The writer has stuck to the assigned topic, and has not made any serious errors in grammar, mechanics, or usage which interfere with the reader's understanding. The essay suffers from somewhat repetitive and uninteresting sen-

tence structure and the occasional use of slang. Proofreading appears to have been careless in some places. Also, some of the evidence provided is general rather than specific.

The introductory paragraph contains the thesis statement, "I agree with the statement that the majority of Americans are overweight and do not exercise enough." This thesis was sufficiently developed in the paragraph, although the sentence structure is occasionally weak. For example, the sentence, "I think that people who are interested in a healthy lifestyle read articles about diet and exercise..." would have been more logically connected with the word "while" than the conjunction "and." Also, the last two sentences in the paragraph contain repetitious sentence structure; they both begin with "this."

In the second paragraph, supporting evidence is given in a overly casual, familiar style which is inappropriate for a formal essay. Furthermore, the statement, "If this is true for me, it must be true for many others as well," is not logical or necessarily true. The following three sentences are repetitious in structure, all beginning with the words, "There is."

The third paragraph contains an error in punctuation, as well as subject and verb agreement. It should read, "The government, as well as many doctors, recommends..." Furthermore, the continued use of an overly casual tone makes the writing appear less literate than it should.

As a conclusion, the final paragraph is weak. It merely restates the thesis without offering any new points or concluding evidence. Since it is only two sentences long, it clearly cannot develop any idea effectively.

Essay Three

On the one hand, I think the statement is true about Americans being overweight. But in some ways its not true. For instants, alot of people diet and exercise you can tell because the gym is always crowded when you want to go and lots of food for sale is fat-free. I don't have to diet because I'm naturally thin but my sister does and she's all ways dieting, but she never stays thin for to long.

But the bad thing, I think is that every time you pick up the newspaper or watch TV they tell you all kinds of contradiction about what you should eat. Sometimes one kind of food is recommended and then the next week they tell you that it causes cancer. Jeez! What are you supposed to beleif? I remember when I was a kid my mother always told me to eat eggs because they are so healthy. But now we know about colesterol so eggs are no good to eat.

So I think that even though we hear all kinds of advice about not getting overweight, its hard for some people not to. And I really think that we should get more exercise. It makes you look better and feel better.

Analysis of Essay Three

This essay scores between 2 and 1. The writer has a weakly stated thesis. It is difficult to discern what the thesis actually is, in fact, without having to refer back to the essay question. The entire essay is marred by faulty grammar, spelling, and usage, and fails to support the main idea with specific examples.

The introductory paragraph contains several misspellings: "instants" should be "instance" and "its" should be "it is;" "alot" is two words, "a lot." The term "all ways" is incorrectly used; the sentence calls for the word "always." Furthermore, the paragraph contains a run-on sentence with faulty parallel structure.

"For instants, alot of people diet and exercise you can tell because the gym is always crowded when you want to go and lots of food for sale is fat-free," should read,

For instance, a lot of people diet and exercise. You can tell because of crowded conditions in gyms, as well as the sale of many types of fat-free foods.

The final sentence in the paragraph needs a comma after "thin," and before "but," and needs to have the preposition "to" changed to the adverb "too."

The inappropriate use of slang in the second paragraph is problematic, making the writing appear less literate than it might have had the writer taken more care. The example about contradictory information lacks specificity (who is "they"?), while the noun "contradiction" should be the adjective "contradictory." Also, the correct spelling of the word in the last sentence of the paragraph is "cholesterol."

In this very weak conclusion, the writer not only neglects to take a clear stand, but actually changes the topic twice, moving from the essay question to the statement that "its [it is] hard for people not to" become overweight. Then the writer abruptly changes the topic once again, to exercise.

Overall, the writer of this essay has rambled without clearly thinking out the topic or providing any supporting evidence.

REVIEW

While you are studying how to improve your writing, your focus should be on the *process* of writing, not the final product. By process, we mean the steps that you and all writers take in moving from a writing assignment to a final draft. These steps include prewriting, or brainstorming to get ideas, outlining the rough draft, writing the first draft, revising, and finally, proofreading for errors. The most important idea to get across to beginning writers

only things that may need to be changed. Perhaps you thought of a better way to say something. It could be that you decide to eliminate part of your piece because it does not seem to belong with the rest of what you have written, or because upon a re-reading, you notice that your logic was faulty, or that you strayed from your original idea. Nothing is ever written in stone, so feel free to experiment until you find the best way to express your ideas.

is that writing should be fluid; it is always in a state of transition, always subject to revision or change until the moment it is handed in. While a piece of writing is *in progress*, the writer has control over the piece, and can make any alterations he or she thinks will improve the final piece.

All too frequently, beginning writers feel that once they have committed pen to paper (or fingers to keyboard) they have to keep what they have written, except for correcting errors. However, any time you write, a second or even third reading is mandatory. Errors are not the

Examine the sample essays at the end of this chapter carefully. Do you get a feel for the clarity and intelligent voice used by the writer of essay one? While reading the second essay, are you aware of ways you might have improved upon some of the weaknesses in sentence structure? Can you find all the errors missed when the writer of essay three proofread the piece? Let the analysis of each essay guide you, but feel free to come up with some revisions of your own. Practice rewriting the second essay. Its format was basically a sound one; it needs only some improvement in sentencing.

Specific Types of Writing

WRITING

SPECIFIC TYPES OF WRITING

THE BUSINESS LETTER

In a personal letter, you may write as informally as you wish, since there are no rules governing its format or contents. Anything goes — as long as the friend to whom you are writing can understand and enjoy your communication. The business letter, however, is a more formal type of writing. It not only must conform to a specific format, but must use a polite, professional tone. Effort must be taken to make sure that you have used appropriate language and that you have communicated your message clearly, without needless confusion.

Business letters are generally written for the following reasons:

- To make a request or complaint

- To reply or confirm a verbal agreement

- To follow up by thanking or reminding someone

- To send inter-office information through memos

Business letters are usually written on a company letterhead and follow a format consisting of six parts.

Return Address — when business stationery is NOT used, the writer's address is placed at the top of the page

Date — date on which the letter was written

Inside Address — name and address of the person to whom the letter is being written

Salutation — "Dear," followed by the person's name, followed by a colon

Body of Letter — contents of letter

Closing and Signature — The standard closing for a business letter is "Very truly yours," or "Sincerely." Then, four or five spaces are skipped and the writer's name is typed below. The writer signs his/her name in between the two typed lines.

In the following business letter, note that the return address and the closing are tabbed to the same margin.

75 S. Jupiter Street
Athens, GA 40401
March 31, 1997

Mr. Jonathan Kotler
Swindlow, Kaplan & O'Shaugnessy
333 Third Avenue
New York City, NY 12200

Dear Mr. Kotler:

Thank you for spending time yesterday to inform me about employment opportunities at your firm. I very much enjoyed talking with you and will give serious consideration to the suggestions you made.

As you requested, I am sending a copy of my resume to the head of your personnel department. I look forward to meeting with you again at your earliest convenience.

Sincerely,

Jeffrey Gordon

Correct format and appropriate language are not the only elements essential to a well-written business letter. Brevity is also important. Business people are busy; if your point is lost in excessive writing, few business executives will have the time or patience to wade through your letter searching for its point. Aim to keep your letter no longer than one page in length. The point of your letter should be clearly stated in the first paragraph. Use the following paragraphs to explain your point.

Clarity is another essential element. Your paragraphs should be short and to the point. Do not fill them with unnecessary details. Provide enough information to make your point clear, and no more. If you have many details, you may wish to set them off in a list instead of using paragraph form.

A concluding paragraph should state what you wish to happen and should include a thank you.

The following example is written on business letterhead and communicates briefly and clearly. Notice that the tone of this letter is polite without being inappropriately familiar.

Groeger, Inc.
1166 Fairview
Tallahassee, FL 33102
August 16, 1996

Ms. Elise D'Artangan
Banquet Manager
Chez Antoine
402 N. Beverly Drive
Beverly Hills, CA 90210

Dear Ms. D'Artangan:

I am writing to confirm the details for the reception we discussed this morning by telephone. As we agreed, Groeger, Inc. will hold its annual corporate shareholders dinner at Chez Antoine on September 27, 1996. The dinner meeting will begin with cocktails and hors d'oeuvres at 7 PM. Dinner should be served by 8 PM. A presentation will follow during coffee and dessert.

The following will provide you a list of what we will need:

• banquet room for 150 guests

• overhead projector and screen

• adequate public address system

• lectern on the dais

Please submit a menu to me no later than next week. I will also need a detailed expense sheet and a confirmation date. I appreciate the effort you are making on behalf of Groeger and look forward to a successful dinner. Thank you for your assistance.

Yours truly,

Helene Walters
Publicity Manager

Rewrite the following letter using appropriate language and format for a business letter.

Question

864 Foxcroft Drive Kalamazoo, MI 41415 June 13, 1996 Mr. Lawrence Edison CarLease, Inc. 815 Portage Road Johnson City, MI 41455 Dear Mr. Edison I want to work for your company. It looks like the kind of place I could get into working for. Your firm needs a person like me — hard working and smart! So, if you want an awesome employee, give me a call. Take care, Danny Hillman

Answer

864 Foxcroft Drive
Kalamazoo, MI 41415
June 13, 1996

Mr. Lawrence Edison
CarLease, Inc.
815 Portage Road
Johnson City, MI 41455

Dear Mr. Edison:

I am writing in response to your advertisement in the <u>Times</u> for a lease manager.

I am quite familiar with CarLease, Inc. and its excellent reputation in the leasing and rental industry from having read numerous articles about the company in <u>Business</u> <u>Week</u> magazine. CarLease offers the hands-on experience I am looking for, in addition to an opportunity for advancement.

After two years at an entry-level position at Dodge Leasing, I believe I can offer the skills necessary to be successful as a lease manager. The enclosed resume details my experiences and skills.

I am a hard-working, self-motivated employee committed to being part of a winning team. I look forward to the opportunity to meet with you to discuss my future at CarLease. I will call you next week to set up an interview at your convenience.

Sincerely,

Daniel Hillman

RESUMES AND JOB APPLICATIONS

Most employers will see your resume before they ever see you! Therefore, a resume is the way most people create a first impression of themselves. Clearly, it is worth your time to use your writing skills to create the right impression. The goal is for your resume to stand out from the others, so that the employer will decide to ask you to come in for an interview.

What, in a resume, creates a positive image of the type of person an employer wants to hire? Most employers would like to hire someone with experience, but are often willing to overlook lack of experience if the resume presents the candidate as being responsible, mature, and self-motivated. While it is inadvisable to be dishonest about your qualifications, there is nothing wrong with making yourself look good by emphasizing your best assets.

To prepare a resume, you will have to think about yourself as objectively as possible. List your personal strengths. Are you a skilled mechanic? Do you enjoy working with people? Is being well-organized a compliment you've been given regularly? If you are having trouble deciding what your personal skills are, ask a friend how he or she would describe you. Listing your personal skills not only helps you focus your resume on the type of employment you are seeking, but will boost your self-confidence as you write.

Organize all the information you have available about your background, especially previous work experience. You will need to include the names and addresses of your previous employers, as well as the positions you held at each job. You must contact at least two people who would be willing to speak favorably about your skills. Once you have obtained their permission, make sure you have their correct names and addresses.

Decide what your career objective is. Employers will not be impressed by an applicant who "wants a job." They want to see an individual who has planned a goal for him/herself within a particular field. What type of work do you want to do? If you are already employed, do you want to switch fields or do you want to advance within the field you are currently in?

EXAMPLES

Objective:
Entry-level position in computer technology

Objective:
Administrative assistant with potential for advancement in music industry

If you have little or no experience, emphasize the skills you already possess which are needed for the position you hope to fill. If you have work experience, be sure to list the responsibilities you have had at each job.

There are several formats you can use for presenting your resume. Decide which format presents your resume best. Regardless of which format you choose, a resume must include the following information:

- Your name, address, and phone number

- Objective — if you are open to several job opportunities, you may want to have several versions of your resume, each with an objective specific to a type of job

- Previous employment, most recent job first

- The names of the schools you attended, the degrees you received, and the dates on which you received them

- Skills pertinent to the job for which you are applying

- Names and addresses of people who have agreed to recommend you, or you may simply write, "references available upon request"

Do not include personal information about your physical appearance, religion, marital status, children, etc. In most situations, it is illegal for an employer to base his/her decision to hire you on any of the above.

You will notice that resumes do not utilize complete sentences, but instead use short phrases to convey the point.

In the resume shown on the following page, the applicant has little work experience, none of which is related to the field she wishes to enter. Therefore, she has emphasized the courses she has taken which will enhance her ability to perform the job well. In the section where she lists her skills, she points out her strengths: being well-organized and dependable.

If you already have some work experience, your resume should list the responsibilities you held at each job. Doing this impresses a potential employer by making him/her aware of your capabilities and demonstrating the confidence your former employers had in you. Choose your verbs carefully when describing your past accomplishments. Aim for words that convey a sense of responsibility and leadership, rather than weak, passive verbs.

NO: did all weekly reports

YES: organized, typed, and disseminated all weekly reports

NO: made employee-of-the-month list several times

YES: consistently appointed to employee-of-the-month list

NO: head typist

YES: supervised typing pool and reported to office manager

Janet Santangelo
457 White Hill Road
Nashua, Massachusetts 04267
617-880-4368

OBJECTIVE

Entry-level position in accounting firm

WORK EXPERIENCE

Typist, Office Temps of Boston. 42 Boylston Street, Boston, MA 05511 June 1993 to present.

EDUCATION

Attended South Side High School. Nashua, MA. 1990-1993.
Attended Adult Education classes to prepare for high school equivalency examination.
  September 1994 to May 1995.
High School Diploma granted June 1995.

SKILLS

Computer literate
Well-organized and able to follow instructions
Self-motivated and dependable

OTHER EXPERIENCE

High school courses in bookkeeping and business mathematics

REFERENCES

Laetitia Bellhaven, chairperson of business education.
South Side High School, Nashua, MA 04267

Edward Finkelstein, office manager. Office Temps of Boston.
42 Boylston Street, Boston, MA 05511

In the following resume, the writer has held several jobs and is looking for a more advanced and higher paying job. Notice how he briefly describes his previous employment.

Darren Hales
35-21 Saunders Street
Forest Hills, NY 11388
718-534-1178

Position wanted: Administrative Assistant in music industry

Work experience: Secretary, WNEW FM radio, NYC, NY
October 1989 to present
- assisted station manager
- scheduled weekly staff meetings
- approved office requisition sheets
- processed and typed staff development reports

Sales clerk, Tower Records, NYC, NY
June 1988 — September 1989
- interacted with customers
- organized stock

Education: Interboro High School, Forest Hills, NY
Diploma granted June 1988

Skills:
- Up-to-date knowledge of music recording industry

- Highly organized and experienced at working in a fast-paced environment

References available upon request

Questions

Rewrite the following phrases to convey a more direct and responsible impression.

1. fixed problems with the photocopier

2. wrote all the staff memos

3. took over when my boss was on vacation

4. ran typing pool

5. put together spreadsheets

6. came up with ideas

7. worked on technological equipment

8. helped department head

9. drew signs for store windows

10. did procedures

Answers

1. "Fixed problems with the photocopier" does not show confidence. "Repaired photocopier when it was malfunctioning" shows confidence, and you possess a capability: You can repair photocopiers. "Repaired" is a stronger verb than "fixed." "Malfunctioning" is more concrete than "problems."

2. "Wrote all the staff memos" does not show confidence. "Initiated all memos" shows

responsibility. "Initiated" is a stronger verb than "wrote."

3. "Took over when my boss was on vacation" does not show confidence. "Assumed the responsibilities of my employer" shows responsibility. "Assumed" is a stronger verb than "took." "Employer" is a stronger term than "boss."

4. "Ran typing pool" does not show confidence. "Managed typing pool" shows leadership and responsibility. You possess a capability: You can manage people. "Managed" is a stronger verb than "ran."

5. "Put together spreadsheets" does not show confidence. "Organized spreadsheets" shows leadership and responsibility. You possess a capability: You can organize. "Organized" is a stronger verb than "put."

6. "Came up with ideas" is too vague and does not show results. "Responsible for developing and researching new approaches and procedures" is more specific and shows more confidence.

7. "Worked on technological equipment" does not show confidence. "Processed technological equipment" shows confidence and responsibility. "Processed" is a stronger verb than "worked."

8. "Helped department head" does not show confidence. "Assisted department head" shows leadership and responsibility. "Assisted" is a stronger verb than "helped."

9. "Drew signs for store windows" does not show confidence. "Designed signs for store windows" shows confidence and responsibility. You possess a capability: You can design a store window display. "Designed" is a stronger verb than "drew."

10. "Did procedures" does not show confidence. "Developed procedures" shows leadership and responsibility. You possess a capability: You can develop a written document. "Developed" is a stronger verb than "did."

JOB APPLICATIONS

A job application is a form which requests most of the information offered on your resume. However, many employers prefer to utilize the job application, since they want specific information that you may not have included on your resume. In addition to asking for you name, address, telephone number, and educational background, job applications generally ask for the following information:

- The position you are applying for. If you are willing to consider a variety of positions, you can write "entry-level position," or "open — depends on opportunity for advancement."

- Salary requirements. Do some research beforehand so you can be prepared for this

question. Find out a typical salary for the position you hope to fill, and based on your own experience and qualifications, request a reasonable wage.

- Social security number. Without a social security number, you cannot legally be employed anywhere in the United States.

- Citizenship. If you are not a U.S. citizen, the interviewer will tell you the company's policies regarding non-citizens.

Even though your resume described your previous work experience, a job application may ask why you left your former employment. It is best not to use personal problems as your reasons for having left a job. If the job was a temporary job, say so. Reasonable answers for having left are "to return to school" or "due to a company's decision to downsize." It is always correct to say that you left in order to seek a better position.

In general, be honest. Potential employers check out the information a candidate puts on the application; misinformation can cost you the job!

☞ **Practice: Job Applications**

DIRECTIONS: Complete the job application on the following pages using the guidelines you have just learned.

APPLICATION FOR EMPLOYMENT

Date of Application _____ / _____ / _____

PERSONAL

Position Applied For: _____

Name _____
FIRST   MIDDLE   LAST

Address _____
NUMBER & STREET   CITY   STATE   ZIP CODE

Telephone (_____) _____ Social Security Number _____ / _____ / _____
AREA CODE

Date of Birth _____ / _____ / _____ Are you employed now? ☐ Yes ☐ No

On what date would you be available for work? _____

EDUCATION

	Elementary	High	College/University	Graduate/Professional
School Name City/State				
Years Completed (circle):	5 6 7 8	9 10 11 12	1 2 3 4	1 2 3 4

Major: _____ Minor: _____

List courses taken: _____ List courses taken: _____

EMPLOYMENT HISTORY

Please give accurate, complete full-time and part-time employment record. Start with present or most recent employer.

1 Company Name	Telephone
Address	Employed (Mo./Yr.) From / to /
Name of Supervisor	Weekly/Annual Pay: Start Last
Job Title and Description of Duties	Reason for Leaving

2 Company Name	Telephone
Address	Employed (Mo./Yr.) From / to /
Name of Supervisor	Weekly/Annual Pay: Start Last
Job Title and Description of Duties	Reason for Leaving

3 Company Name	Telephone
Address	Employed (Mo./Yr.) From / to /
Name of Supervisor	Weekly/Annual Pay: Start Last
Job Title and Description of Duties	Reason for Leaving

We may contact the employers listed above unless you indicate those you do not want us to contact.

Do not contact (indicate employer by number) _____

Reason _____

PLEASE SEE OVER AND COMPLETE SECOND SIDE.

151

ADDITIONAL INFORMATION

━━━━━━━━━━━ **VOLUNTARY** ━━━━━━━━━━━

Marital Status: Date of Marriage _____

☐ Single   ☐ Engaged   ☐ Married

☐ Separated   ☐ Divorced   ☐ Widowed   Number of children

Are you a U.S. Citizen?   ☐ Yes   ☐ No

Have you been convicted of a crime in the past ten years, excluding misdemeanors and summary offenses, which has not been annulled, expunged or sealed by a court?

☐ Yes   ☐ No

If yes, please describe in full: _____

_____

Related coursework:

SIGNATURE

The information provided in this Application for Employment is true, correct and complete. If employed, any misstatement or omission of fact on this application may result in my dismissal.

I understand that acceptance of an offer of employment does not create a contractual obligation upon the employer to continue to employ me in the future.

If you decide to engage an investigative consumer reporting agency to report on my credit and personal history, I authorize you to do so. If a report is obtained you must provide, at my request, the name and address of the agency so I may obtain from them the nature and substance of the information contained in the report.

_____   _____
            Date   Signature of Applicant

APPLICATION FOR EMPLOYMENT

Date of Application __February 2__

PERSONAL

Position Applied For: __Full charge bookkeeper__

Name __Lloyd__ __Jason__ __Carson__
FIRST   MIDDLE   LAST

Address __16__ __Meadowlark Way__, __Cranford, NY__ __08816__
NUMBER & STREET   CITY   STATE   ZIP CODE

Telephone __(201)__ __743 - 9972__ Social Security Number __975 / 44 / 16622__
AREA CODE

Date of Birth __10 / 14 / 71__ Are you employed now? ☑ Yes ☐ No

On what date would you be available for work? __end of February__

EDUCATION

		Elementary	High	College/University	Graduate/Professional
School Name City/State		River Road Elementary School Succasaunna, NJ	Regional High School Dover, NJ	Herbert H. Lehman college /CUNY NYC, NY	
Years Completed (circle):		5 6 7 (8)	9 10 11 (12)	1 (2) 3 4	1 2 3 4

Major: __Business Administration__   Minor: __Accounting__

List courses taken: __business math, Intro to Law__   List courses taken: __Accounting 101, 220__

EMPLOYMENT HISTORY

Please give accurate, complete full-time and part-time employment record. Start with present or most recent employer.

1.	
Company Name __Bergen County Employees Credit Union__	Telephone __201 - 847 - 4747__
Address __1050 Forbell Street Suite 125__ Paramus NJ	Employed (Mo./Yr.) From __6 /94__ to __present__
Name of Supervisor __Leslie Bissell__	Weekly/(Annual) Pay: Start __25 thous__ Last __30 thous__
Job Title and Description of Duties __Bookkeeper - Senior__ __bank recs, payroll, account analysis, journal entries__	Reason for Leaving __to seek a better position__

2	
Company Name __Paymer Metal Works__	Telephone __201 - 776 - 1400__
Address __2020 Bergenfield Rd. Hackensack NJ.__	Employed (Mo./Yr.) From __8 /91__ to __5 /94__
Name of Supervisor __David Charles, Jr.__	Weekly/(Annual) Pay: Start __22__ Last __25 thousan__
Job Title and Description of Duties __assistant bookkeeper__ __payroll, data entry, collections + credit__	Reason for Leaving __I wanted to work in a larger firm with more opportunity for advancement__

3	
Company Name __Russell William, Inc__	Telephone __609 - 249 - 9400__
Address __1710 midway Road Oceantown, NJ__	Employed (Mo./Yr.) From __6 /90__ to __8 /91__
Name of Supervisor __martha Greene__	(Weekly)/Annual Pay: Start Last __$200__
Job Title and Description of Duties __Administrative Asst__ __payroll, office management, some secty. duties__	Reason for Leaving __temporary job while in college__

We may contact the employers listed above unless you indicate those you do not want us to contact.

Do not contact (indicate employer by number) __You may contact any of the above__

Reason _____

> **PLEASE SEE OVER AND COMPLETE SECOND SIDE.**

OPTIONAL

Marital Status:

☒ Single ☐ Engaged ☐ Married

☐ Separated ☐ Divorced ☐ Widowed

Date of Marriage _____

Number of children _____

Are you a U.S. Citizen?

☒ Yes ☐ No

Have you been convicted of a crime in the past ten years, excluding misdemeanors and summary offenses, which has not been annulled, expunged or sealed by a court?

☐ Yes ☒ No

If yes, please describe in full: _____

_____

Related coursework:

Computer Applications for Lotus and Word Perfect

Financial Analysis

Spanish - 4 years in high school and college

The information provided in this Application for Employment is true, correct and complete. If employed, any mistatement or omission of fact on this application may result in my dismissal.

I understand that acceptance of an offer of employment does not create a contractual obligation upon the employer to continue to employ me in the future.

If you decide to engage an investigative consumer reporting agency to report on my credit and personal history, I authorize you to do so. If a report is obtained you must provide, at my request, the name and address of the agency so I may obtain from them the nature and substance of the information contained in the report.

February 2

_____
Date

Lloyd J. Carson

_____
Signature

REVIEW

When people meet you face to face, they have a chance to get to know you. While appearances, especially first appearances, are important, personal contact affords you the opportunity to develop the impression you wish to give a potential employer. Even if the impression you initially give is less than ideal, you can quickly correct any misunderstanding and secure the position you were seeking. The key to gaining access to a personal interview, however, is through writing; the image you portray in your resume and cover letter is essential to being granted an interview, and ultimately, a job. Therefore, no corners can be cut, nor careless mistakes made when preparing business-related writing. The impression made by means of your written communication may be the only impression you make.

As we have stressed throughout this chapter, the key element in business writing is a professional tone. Care must be taken to strike the correct balance between sounding pretentious and stuffy or immature and careless. A professional tone is one which aims for polite-ness and clarity. Your intention in writing should be obvious, not vague, and all information should be clearly stated in a logical manner. Furthermore, you should not sound friendly, as if you already know the person with whom you are seeking an interview, nor should you be stiffly formal. Remember, the point of business writing is to do business; use your letter or resume to convey the impression that you are capable and confident of doing the job.

Once you are successfully employed, many jobs will call for you to continue using your writing skills. Even if your job does not require you to initiate any writing, you may need to perform editing tasks, especially if you take shorthand or type the correspondence of others. An employee who can find and correct errors before his or her boss sends out a letter or a memo will be valued above the rest. Additionally, there is little hope for advancement within a company unless your work is of superior quality. Developing a reputation for excellence in proofreading and writing can only prove beneficial. Therefore, for those who are motivated to get ahead, learning to write well is a skill worth acquiring.

Post-Test

WRITING

POST-TEST

DIRECTIONS: Read each of the sentences below and then choose the answer choice which best corrects the underlined portion of the sentence.

1. The children swam in the lake all day <u>and that is because it was so hot.</u>

   (1) and that is because it was so hot.

   (2) when it was so hot.

   (3) since it was so hot.

   (4) which is why it was so hot.

   (5) at the time when it was so hot.

2. That some serious cuts would have to be made in the city's budget <u>was evident to most everyone on the city council.</u>

   (1) was evident to most everyone on the city council.

   (2) was in evidence to most all on the city council.

   (3) was evident to almost everyone on the city council.

   (4) was evidenced by most everyone on the city council.

   (5) was evidencing to almost everyone on the city council.

3. When a customer requested whole wheat instead of white bread, <u>it was a simple matter to substitute it for them.</u>

   (1) it was a simple matter to substitute it for them.

   (2) it was a simple matter to substitute it.

   (3) a simple matter it was to make the substitution.

   (4) substitution was made a simple matter for him or her.

   (5) it was easy to serve him or her.

4. <u>This morning's meeting having gone well</u> because Mrs. Chen was prepared with information to answer all our questions.

   (1) This morning's meeting having gone well

   (2) This morning's meeting having gone good

   (3) The meeting of this morning went good

   (4) This morning's meeting went well

   (5) This meeting in the morning going well

5. During the summer, <u>Josh developed his skill in both diving and to swim.</u>

(1) Josh developed his skill in both diving and to swim.

(2) Josh developed his skills both to dive and in swimming.

(3) Josh developed his skills in both diving and swimming.

(4) Josh developed his skills in swimming and to dive.

(5) Josh developed his skills as a diver and to swim.

6. In order to keep track of his <u>costs, a detailed diary was kept by the salesman for his automobile expenses</u>.

(1) cost, a detailed diary was kept by the salesman for his automobile expenses.

(2) costs; a detailed diary was kept by the salesman for his automobile expenses.

(3) automobile expenses, the salesman kept a detailed diary.

(4) expenses for his automobile, a detailed costs diary was kept by the salesman.

(5) automobile expenses, the salesman kept a detailed diary of the costs.

7. After the storm, we were told <u>to leave the tree laying</u> on the house until the insurance inspector came.

(1) to leave the tree laying

(2) to leave the tree lay

(3) about leaving the tree to lay

(4) about leaving the tree lying

(5) to leave the tree lying

8. The judges at the fair all agreed that our one-act play <u>was crisp, witty, and the cast was talented</u>.

(1) was crisp, witty, and the cast was talented.

(2) was very crisp, very witty, and the cast was very talented.

(3) seemed crisp and witty and talented.

(4) appeared crisp; witty; and the cast was talented.

(5) was crisp, witty, and had a talented cast.

9. Because the two contestants are so evenly matched, <u>it is difficult for me deciding which one to receive the trophy</u>.

(1) it is difficult for me deciding which one to receive the trophy.

(2) it is difficult for me deciding which one to give the trophy to.

(3) it is difficult for me to decide to whom to give the trophy.

(4) I am having difficulty deciding who should receive the trophy.

(5) I am having difficulty deciding whom should receive the trophy.

10. Frankly, <u>I'd like to keep this confidential between you and I</u>.

(1) I'd like to keep this confidential between you and I.

(2) I'd like to keep this confidential between you and me.

(3) I'd like to keep this confidential between we people.

(4) we should keep this confidential between you and I.

(5) I'd like to keep this confidentially between you and I.

11. Construction jobs <u>performed by him and his partner</u> are always late.

   (1) performed by him and his partner

   (2) performed by his partner and him

   (3) that him and his partner performed

   (4) performed by he and his partner

   (5) performed by them

12. <u>Several of our group is going</u> to participate in this event.

   (1) Several of our group is going

   (2) Several of our group is going to go

   (3) Several of our group are going

   (4) Several of our group is going to be going

   (5) Several in our group is going

13. In fact, <u>there the best</u> in the business.

   (1) there the best

   (2) they're the best

   (3) there the bestest

   (4) they're the most best

   (5) there the most best

14. <u>I thought I knew the poem by heart, but she showed me two lines I had missed</u>.

   (1) I thought I knew the poem by heart, but she showed me two lines I had missed.

   (2) I thought, I knew the poem by heart, but she showed me two lines I thought I had missed.

   (3) I thought I knew the poem by heart but, she showed me two lines I had missed.

   (4) I thought I knew, the poem by heart, but she showed me two lines I had missed.

   (5) I thought I knew the poem by heart, but she showed me, two lines I had missed.

15. Frank was worried about his daughter's adjustment to school, <u>but she took to it real well</u>.

   (1) but she took to it real well.

   (2) but she took to it real good.

   (3) but she took to it really good.

   (4) but she took to it really well.

   (5) but she took it real well.

16. <u>Both of us hopes and prays</u> everything will turn out well.

   (1) Both of us hopes and prays

   (2) Both of us hope and prays

   (3) Both of us, we hope and pray

   (4) Both of us, we hopes and prays

   (5) Both of us hope and pray

17. <u>Many of his songs were romantic and sentimental</u>.

   (1) Many of his songs were romantic and sentimental.

   (2) Many of his songs was romantic and sentimental.

   (3) Many of his songs were romantic, and sentimental.

   (4) Many of his songs was romantic, and sentimental.

(5) Many of his songs were romantic; sentimental.

18. <u>People that play with fire</u> should expect to get burned.

   (1) People that play with fire

   (2) People, playing with fire

   (3) People which play with fire

   (4) People who play with fire

   (5) People whom play with fire

19. <u>All of the secretaries and the office manager threatens</u> to quit if the heating isn't fixed.

   (1) All of the secretaries and the office manager threatens

   (2) All of the secretaries and the office manager threaten

   (3) All of the secretaries and the office manager threatens

   (4) All of the secretaries and the office manager, threaten

   (5) All of the secretaries and the office manager, threatens

20. Filene's has a wonderful sale <u>on childrens' jackets</u>.

   (1) on childrens' jackets.

   (2) about childrens' jackets.

   (3) on children's jackets.

   (4) on childrens jackets.

   (5) on childs' jackets.

21. <u>To often</u>, people jump to unfair conclusions.

   (1) To often,

   (2) Two often,

   (3) To often

   (4) Too often,

   (5) Too often

22. <u>Everyone in the show brought their</u> scripts and costumes.

   (1) Everyone in the show brought their

   (2) Everyone in the show brought themselves

   (3) Everyone in the show brought his or her

   (4) Everyone in the show brought they're

   (5) Everyone in the show brought his or hers

23. When she unintentionally hurt Corry's feelings, <u>Harriet felt badly for days</u>.

   (1) Harriet felt badly for days.

   (2) Harriet was feeling badly for days.

   (3) Harriet felt bad for days.

   (4) Harriet had felt badly for days.

   (5) Harriet felt bad, for days.

24. <u>Frank fixed the copy machine by hisself</u>.

   (1) Frank fixed the copy machine by hisself.

   (2) Frank fixed the copy machine, by hisself.

   (3) Frank fixed the copy machine, by himself.

   (4) Frank hisself fixed the copy machine.

   (5) Frank fixed the copy machine by himself.

25. <u>The reason being they never got along.</u>

    (1) The reason being they never got along.

    (2) The reason for their breakup was that they never got along.

    (3) The reason for their breakup being they never got along.

    (4) The reason for their breakup were they never got along.

    (5) The reason not being they never got along.

26. The itinerary for Gail and Steve's vacation includes <u>Paris France, London England, Madrid Spain.</u>

    (1) Paris France, London England, Madrid Spain.

    (2) Paris France, London England, and Madrid Spain.

    (3) Paris, France, London, England, and Madrid, Spain.

    (4) Paris, France; London, England; Madrid, Spain.

    (5) Paris, France, London, England, Madrid, Spain.

27. <u>Robbie and Pam took a summer trip, Brian and Peter stayed home.</u>

    (1) Robbie and Pam took a summer trip, Brian and Peter stayed home.

    (2) Robbie and Pam took a summer trip, but Brian and Peter stayed home.

    (3) Robbie and Pam, took a summer trip, Brian and Peter stayed home.

    (4) Robbie and Pam took a summer trip:
    Brian and Peter stayed home.

    (5) Robbie and Pam took a summer trip but Brian and Peter stayed home.

28. Jason told LaShone, <u>"You can't be doing that here."</u>

    (1) "You can't be doing that here."

    (2) "You dasn't do that here."

    (3) "You can't do that here."

    (4) You can't do that here.

    (5) "You can not be doing that here."

29. <u>Dan saw his missing cat driving down Broadway.</u>

    (1) Dan saw his missing cat driving down Broadway.

    (2) Dan saw his missing cat, driving down Broadway.

    (3) Driving down Broadway, Dan saw his missing cat.

    (4) Driving down Broadway Dan saw his missing cat.

    (5) Dan saw his missing cat and was driving down Broadway.

30. Francine's ability to spell was always <u>approximate</u>.

    (1) approximate.

    (2) aproximate.

    (3) approximately.

    (4) aproximately.

    (5) to be approximate.

DIRECTIONS: Choose the <u>one best answer</u> to correct the sentence.

31. The coach knowed Kendrick's parents couldn't afford to send him to college.

    (1) noo
    (2) knows
    (3) be knowing
    (4) nowed
    (5) no correction

32. Getting ready for a test all ways involves a lot of preparation.

    (1) change "preparation" to "perperation"
    (2) put a colon after "test"
    (3) change "all ways" to "always"
    (4) change "preparation" to "preparing"
    (5) no correction

33. When I go to the movies, me and my wife share the popcorn.

    (1) remove the comma after "movies"
    (2) change "me and my wife" to "my wife and me"
    (3) change "me and my wife" to "my wife and myself"
    (4) change "me and my wife" to "my wife and I"
    (5) no correction

34. Several of the students is going to enroll for the summer film series.

    (1) change "enroll" to "enrol"
    (2) add a comma after "students"
    (3) change "is going" to "are going"

(4) change "summer" to "summer's"
(5) no correction

35. If you know how to dress for the occasion, you'll feel much more comfortable.

    (1) change "know" to "now"
    (2) remove the comma after "occasion"
    (3) change "comfortable" to "comftible"
    (4) change "you'll" to "youl"
    (5) no correction

36. To often, people misjudge each other based on appearances.

    (1) change "To often" to "Too often"
    (2) remove the comma after "often"
    (3) change "misjudge" to "missjudge"
    (4) change "misjudge" to "misjudges"
    (5) no correction

37. Few of us except the fact that our parents are getting older.

    (1) change "parents" to "parent's"
    (2) change "are getting" to "is getting"
    (3) add a comma after "fact"
    (4) change "except" to "accept"
    (5) no correction

38. Never give away any recipes belonging to Grandma and I.

    (1) change "Grandma and I" to "Grandma and myself"
    (2) change "Grandma and I" to "Grandma and me"
    (3) change "recipes" to "recepes"

(4) change "never give" to "never be giving"

(5) no correction

39. Brenda, whom is a teacher at my school, likes romantic poetry.

    (1) remove the comma after "school"

    (2) remove the comma after "Brenda"

    (3) change "whom" to "who"

    (4) change "likes" to "is liking"

    (5) no correction

40. Both of them work at jobs after class.

    (1) change "work" to "works"

    (2) add a comma after "them"

    (3) change "at jobs" to "to jobs"

    (4) change "work" to "are working"

    (5) no correction

41. My flight to the Dominican Republic was on a boeing 747.

    (1) change "boeing" to "Boeing"

    (2) change "Dominican Republic" to "Dominican republic"

    (3) change "Dominican Republic" to "dominican Republic"

    (4) change "747" to "seven hundred forty-seven.

    (5) no correction

42. All of us were sorry to hear that Yolanda's mother past away.

    (1) change "were sorry" to "was sorry"

    (2) change "hear" to "here"

    (3) remove the apostrophe from "Yolanda's"

(4) change "past" to "passed"

(5) no correction

43. Flora really wants to lose some weight but she can't seem to control her eating.

    (1) change "weight" to "wait"

    (2) change "wants" to "want"

    (3) add a comma after "weight"

    (4) add a comma after "lose"

    (5) no correction

44. Ashton, Oklahoma is the most ugly city I have ever seen.

    (1) remove the comma after "Ashton"

    (2) change "most ugly" to "most ugliest"

    (3) change "most ugly" to "ugliest"

    (4) change "most ugly" to "most ugliest"

    (5) no correction

45. I bought a dress walking down the street.

    (1) add "while" after "dress"

    (2) add a comma after "dress"

    (3) add a comma after "walking"

    (4) add the words "and I was" after "dress"

    (5) no correction

46. All of these styles are soon to be outdated.

    (1) add a comma after "All"

    (2) change "are" to "is"

    (3) change "these" to "these here"

    (4) add a comma after "styles"

    (5) no correction

47. Several times a week, I take a class which is really boaring.

    (1) change " really" to "real"

    (2) remove the comma after "week"

    (3) change "which" to "what"

    (4) change "boaring" to "boring"

    (5) no correction

48. The site of you makes me go weak in the knees.

    (1) change "weak" to "week"

    (2) change "knees" to "niece"

    (3) change "site" to "sight"

    (4) change "makes" to "make"

    (5) no correction

49. The entire class, especially Nola and Michelle, were thrilled when the exam was cancelled.

    (1) change "were" to "was"

    (2) remove the comma after "Michelle"

    (3) change "cancelled" to "canceled"

    (4) change "when the exam was cancelled" to "for the exam to be cancelled."

    (5) no correction

50. <u>The baked ziti was served on large platters to the guests.</u>

    (1) The baked ziti was served to the guests on large platters.

    (2) The baked ziti, was served on large platters to the guests.

    (3) The baked ziti was served, to the guests on large platters.

    (4) To the guests was served baked ziti on large platters.

    (5) no correction

51. Since Deena and Jackie are waiting.

    (1) Since Deena and Jackie, are waiting.

    (2) Since Deena and Jackie is waiting.

    (3) Since Deena and Jackie are waiting, and Perri and Leah are also.

    (4) Since Deena and Jackie are waiting, someone should go to get them.

    (5) no correction

52. <u>No one who last saw Halley's comet is alive today.</u>

    (1) No one who last saw halley's comet is alive today.

    (2) No one, who last saw Halley's comet is alive today.

    (3) No one who last saw Halley's Comet is alive today.

    (4) No one who last saw Halley's comet, is alive today.

    (5) no correction

53. <u>Vera grew sadly at the thought of losing her job.</u>

    (1) Vera grew sadly at the thought of loosing her job.

    (2) Vera growed sadly at the thought of losing her job.

    (3) Vera grew sad at the thought of losing her job.

    (4) Vera grew sad, at the thought of losing her job.

    (5) no correction

54. <u>Pies baked by she and her daughter are always flaky.</u>

    (1) Pies baked by she and her daughter are all ways flaky.

    (2) Pies baked by her and her daughter are always flaky.

    (3) Pies baked by she and her daughter is always flaky.

    (4) Pies baked by herself and her daughter are always flaky

    (5) no correction

55. <u>Serious fans of musical's will adore "Bring in da Noise, Bring in da Funk."</u>

    (1) Serious fan's of musical's will adore "Bring in da Noise, Bring in da Funk."

    (2) Serious fans of musicals will adore "Bring in da Noise, bring in da Funk."

    (3) Serious fans of musical's will adore Bring in da Noise, bring in da Funk.

    (4) Serious fans of musical's will adore: "Bring in da Noise, Bring in da Funk."

    (5) no correction

WRITING
POST-TEST
ANSWER KEY

1. (3)	15. (4)	29. (3)	43. (3)
2. (3)	16. (5)	30. (1)	44. (3)
3. (2)	17. (1)	31. (2)	45. (1)
4. (4)	18. (4)	32. (3)	46. (5)
5. (3)	19. (2)	33. (4)	47. (4)
6. (5)	20. (3)	34. (3)	48. (3)
7. (5)	21. (4)	35. (5)	49. (1)
8. (5)	22. (3)	36. (1)	50. (5)
9. (4)	23. (3)	37. (4)	51. (4)
10. (2)	24. (5)	38. (2)	52. (5)
11. (4)	25. (2)	39. (3)	53. (3)
12. (3)	26. (4)	40. (5)	54. (2)
13. (2)	27. (2)	41. (1)	55. (2)
14. (1)	28. (3)	42. (4)	

POST-TEST SELF-EVALUATION

Question Number	Subject Matter Tested	Section to Study (section, heading)
1.	Sentence Structure	Sentence Structure, compound sentences
2.	Modifiers	Modifying Words, adjectives, and adverbs
3.	Pronouns	Pronouns, types of pronouns
4.	Sentence Structure	Sentence Structure, compound sentences
4.	Verbs	Verbs, tenses
4.	Modifiers	Modifying Words, adjectives and adverbs
5.	Sentence Structure	Sentence Structure, compound sentences
6.	Sentence Structure	Sentence Structure, compound sentences
7.	Spelling	Spelling, hints for correct spelling
8.	Punctuation	Punctuation, commas
9.	Verbs	Verbs, tenses
9.	Pronouns	Pronouns, relative pronouns
10.	Pronouns	Pronouns, types of pronouns
11.	Pronouns	Pronouns, types of pronouns
12.	Nouns	Nouns, collective nouns
12.	Subject/Verb Agreement	Subject/Verb Agreement, agreement
13.	Spelling	Spelling, homonyms
14.	Punctuation	Punctuation, commas
15.	Modifiers	Modifying Words, adjectives and adverbs
16.	Subject/Verb Agreement	Subject/Verb Agreement, agreement
17.	Subject/Verb Agreement	Subject/Verb Agreement, agreement

Question Number	Subject Matter Tested	Section to Study (section, heading)
18.	Pronouns	Pronouns, relative pronouns
19.	Subject/Verb Agreement	Subject/Verb Agreement, agreement
20.	Nouns	Nouns, forming the plural of nouns
21.	Spelling	Spelling, homonyms
22.	Spelling	Spelling, homonyms
22.	Subject/Verb Agreement	Subject/Verb Agreement, agreement
23.	Modifiers	Modifying Words, adjectives and adverbs
24.	Pronouns	Pronouns, reflexive pronouns
25.	Sentence Structure	Sentence Structure, compound sentences
25.	Subject/Verb Agreement	Subject/Verb Agreement, agreement
26.	Punctuation	Punctuation, commas
27.	Punctuation	Punctuation, commas
27.	Sentence Structure	Sentence Structure, compound sentences
28.	Punctuation	Punctuation, quotation marks
29.	Sentence Structure	Sentence Structure, compound sentences
30.	Modifiers	Modifying Words, adjectives and adverbs
30.	Spelling	Spelling, hints for correct spelling
31.	Spelling	Spelling, hints for correct spelling
31.	Verbs	Verbs, tenses
32.	Spelling	Spelling, hints for correct spelling
33.	Pronouns	Pronouns, types of pronouns
34.	Subject/Verb Agreement	Subject/Verb Agreement, agreement

Question Number	Subject Matter Tested	Section to Study (section, heading)
35.	Spelling	Spelling, hints for correct spelling
36.	Spelling	Spelling, homonyms
37.	Spelling	Spelling, homonyms
38.	Spelling	Spelling, hints for correct spelling
39.	Pronouns	Pronouns, relative pronouns
40.	Subject/Verb Agreement	Subject/Verb Agreement, agreement
41.	Capitalization	Capitalization, names of ships, aircraft
42.	Subject/Verb Agreement	Subject/Verb Agreement, agreement
43.	Spelling	Spelling, homonyms
44.	Spelling	Modifying Words, adjectives and adverbs
45.	Sentence Structure	Sentence Structure, compound sentences
46.	Verbs	Verbs, tenses
47.	Spelling	Spelling, hints for correct spelling
48.	Spelling	Spelling, hints for correct spelling
49.	Verbs	Verbs, subject/verb agreement
50.	Sentence Structure	Sentence Structure, compound sentences
51.	Sentence Structure	Sentence Structure, compound sentences
52.	Capitalization	Capitalization, names of astronomical bodies
53.	Modifiers	Modifying Words, adjectives and adverbs
54.	Pronouns	Pronouns, types of pronouns
55.	Nouns	Nouns, types of nouns

POST-TEST
ANSWERS AND EXPLANATIONS

1. **(3)** The word "since" explains logically why the children swam all day. Choices (1) and (5) are non-parallel clauses. Choices (2) and (4) are not logical.

2. **(3)** Only choices (1) and (3) use the required adjective form "evidence." (1) misuses "most" instead of "almost."

3. **(2)** (1) is incorrect, since the subject "customer" is singular and the pronoun "them" is plural. (3) is too wordy. (4) is too awkward, even though it correctly uses singular pronouns, "him or her."

4. **(4)** The first two choices use the verb incorrectly. (3) uses an adjective instead of an adverb. (5) is a fragment.

5. **(3)** None of the other choices have parallel structure.

6. **(5)** Choice (3) doesn't give complete information about what type of diary the salesman kept. Choices (1) and (2) use the incorrect preposition, "for," instead of "of." (2) also misuses the semicolon. (4) is incorrect because the word "costs" is incorrectly used as an adjective.

7. **(5)** The other choices all misuse the verb "to lay."

8. **(5)** None of the other choices has parallel structure.

9. **(4)** Choices (1) and (2) use an incorrect form of the verb "decide." (3) is too wordy. (5) incorrectly uses the object pronoun "whom."

10. **(2)** All the other choices incorrectly use subject pronouns following the preposition "between."

11. **(4)** All the other choices incorrectly use object pronouns where a subject pronoun is required.

12. **(3)** "Several" is a plural indefinite pronoun. All the other choices use a singular form of the verb "is"; therefore, only (3) has subject and verb agreement.

13. **(2)** "There" is an adverb. The sentence clearly is meant to refer to the subject "they." Since "they're" is often confused with "there," choices (1), (3), and (5) are incorrect. (3), (4), and (5) also misuse superlative forms of the adjective "good."

14. **(1)** All the other choices have incorrect comma placement. In (1), the comma separates the main clause from the dependent clause by placing the comma before the conjunction, "but."

15. **(4)** The verb "took" requires an adverb to modify it. "Well" is an adverb, but "good" is an adjective, making (2) and (3) incorrect. An adverb can only be modified by another adverb; "really" is an adverb, while "real" is an adjective. Choices (1), (2), and (5) all use "real" instead of "really."

16. **(5)** "Both" is a plural indefinite pronoun, therefore the verb must agree by being in a plural form as well. Choices (1), (2), and (4) use at least one singular verb. (3) is incor-

rect because it has an unnecessary comma separating the subject and the verb.

17. **(1)**   Since "many" is a plural indefinite pronoun, the verb must agree by being in a plural form as well. (2) and (4) use a singular form of the verb. (3) and (5) use incorrect punctuation to separate the compound direct objects, "romantic and sentimental."

18. **(4)**   Choice (2) is missing a relative pronoun and has an unnecessary comma separating the subject from the verb. (1) and (3) use pronouns meant to refer to things, not to people. (5) incorrectly uses an object pronoun for a subject pronoun.

19. **(2)**   When one part of a compound subject is plural and the other is singular, the verb must agree with the subject closest to it. Since "office manager" is nearest to the verb and is singular, choices (1), (3), and (5) are wrong because they use plural forms of the verb. (4) and (5) have unnecessary commas separating the subject and the verb.

20. **(3)**   The correct way to form the possessive of the plural noun "children" is to add "'s" to the word.

21. **(4)**   "To," "too," and "two" are often confused. The sentence requires an adverb, "too," to show to what extent people jump to conclusions. Neither (1), (2), nor (3) use the adverb. (5) omits the necessary comma.

22. **(3)**   "Everyone" is a singular indefinite pronoun. (1) uses a plural possessive pronoun, so the sentence lacks agreement. (2) uses a reflexive pronoun instead of a possessive. (4) uses the contraction of the subject and verb "they are" instead of a pronoun. (5) uses a plural possessive pronoun.

23. **(3)**   The verb "felt" is a linking verb in

this sentence; therefore, it needs a predicate adjective, not an adverb, to modify the subject. (1) and (2) use an adverb. (4) changes the tense of the verb unnecessarily. (5) includes an unnecessary comma.

24. **(5)**   Choices (1), (2), and (4) use a non-existent reflexive pronoun, "hisself." (3) has an unnecessary comma.

25. **(2)**   Choices (1), (3), and (5) are sentence fragments. (4) uses a plural form of the verb in a sentence with a singular subject.

26. **(4)**   Cities are always separated from their countries by a comma. In a list of cities and their countries, the countries are then separated by a semicolon.

27. **(2)**   (1) is a run-on. (3) and (4) have unnecessary punctuation. (5) lacks any punctuation.

28. **(3)**   Choice (4) is missing quotation marks. (2) contains a non-existent word, "dasn't." (1) and (5) both incorrectly use the verb "be" along with the verb "doing."

29. **(3)**   Choices (1) and (2) have misplaced modifiers. (4) is missing the comma needed to separate the dependent clause from the main clause. (5) is awkward and illogical.

30. **(1)**   The adjective "approximate" modifies the noun "ability." (3) and (4) use an adverb, not an adjective. (2) and (4) are misspelled. (5) is too wordy.

31. **(2)**   "Knows" uses the correct verb form— the present simple. (1) and (4) are misspelled words. The verb form of (3) is nonstandard English.

32. **(3)**   "All ways" is a misspelling. (2) is incorrect since a colon must be preceded by a

complete sentence. (1) is a misspelling. (4) is incorrect since the sentence requires a noun form of the word, not the gerund, "preparing."

33. **(4)** Since "my wife and I" is the compound subject of the sentence, it requires a subject pronoun, "I." (2) and (3) use incorrect pronouns; (2) uses an object pronoun; and (3) uses a reflexive. (1) is incorrect since a comma is needed to separate the dependent clause from the main clause.

34. **(3)** The indefinite pronoun "several" is plural and must agree with the verb "are," not "is." (1) is a misspelling. (2) is incorrect since it places a comma between the subject and the verb. (4) is incorrect because it changes the noun "summer" to a possessive.

35. **(5)** The sentence is correct. (1), (3), and (4) involve misspellings. The comma in (2) is necessary to separate the dependent clause from the main clause.

36. **(1)** "To" is a preposition; "too" is the adverb needed to modify the adverb "often," showing to what extent people misjudge each other. (3) and (4) are misspellings. The comma in (2) is needed to separate the dependent clause from the main clause.

37. **(4)** "Except" means to leave out, so the word "accept," meaning to agree to something, is needed. (1) is incorrect since it changes the noun "parents" to a possessive. (2) is incorrect because the subject, "parents," doesn't agree with the verb "is." (3) is incorrect because the comma has no purpose in the sentence.

38. **(2)** "Me" is an object pronoun, and the preposition "to" must be followed by an object. (1) incorrectly uses a reflexive pronoun. (3) is a misspelled word. (4) uses a verb form found only in non-standard English.

39. **(3)** The phrase "who is a teacher at my school" is an appositive phrase modifying the subject, "Brenda," so the subject pronoun "who" must be used. (1) and (2) are incorrect because commas are necessary to separate an appositive phrase from the remainder of the sentence. (4) uses a verb form found only in non-standard English.

40. **(5)** The sentence is correct. (1) would cause the subject and verb not to agree. Adding a comma (2) separates the subject and the verb. (3) is wrong because it uses an incorrect preposition. (4) is incorrect because the progressive form of a verb is not used for an action which is repeated on a daily basis.

41. **(1)** Names of aircraft are capitalized. (2) and (3) are wrong since names of countries are capitalized. (4) is incorrect since numbers over 100 are expressed in numerals, not words.

42. **(4)** "Past" refers to something that has already happened; "passed," the past tense of "to pass," correctly expresses the idea that Yolanda's mother has died. (1) is wrong because the subject and verb no longer agree. (2) replaces the adverb "here" with the verb "hear." (3) is incorrect since the apostrophe is needed to show that the mother belonged to Yolanda.

43. **(3)** The comma is needed before the conjunction "but." (4) is wrong because a comma there would disrupt the meaning of the sentence. (1) is incorrect because it confuses the noun "weight" with the verb "wait." (2) is incorrect because the subject and verb no longer agree.

44. **(3)** The superlative form of the adjective "ugly" is "ugliest." (2) and (4) are incorrect comparative adverb forms. The comma (1) is needed since a comma always separates a town and its state.

45. **(1)** The addition of the word "while" corrects the sentence's misplaced modifier. (2) and (3) are wrong since a comma would confuse the meaning of the sentence. (4) is incorrect because it creates a sentence with two unrelated clauses.

46. **(5)** The sentence is correct. (1) and (4) are wrong since a comma would confuse the meaning of the sentence. (2) is incorrect since the indefinite pronoun "All" is plural, and needs to agree with the verb "are," not "is."

47. **(4)** "Boaring" is a misspelled word. (1) is wrong because "real" is an adjective, and only an adverb (really) can modify an adjective (boring). The comma (2) is needed to separate the dependent clause from the main clause. (3) uses an incorrect relative pronoun.

48. **(3)** "Site" and "sight" are homonyms; "sight" is the correct word in this sentence. (1) and (2) use incorrect homonyms. (4) changes the subject and verb agreement.

49. **(1)** The subject of the sentence is "class," which must agree with the verb "was," not "were." The comma (2) is needed to complete the separation between the dependent clause and the main clause. (3) is a misspelled word. (4) is incorrect since the sentence would be too wordy.

50. **(5)** The sentence is correct. (1) misplaces the modifier "on large platters." (2) and (3) are incorrect since they add commas which separate the subject and the verb. (4) changes

the subject and verb agreement; "guests" is the subject. The verb "was" does not agree.

51. **(4)** This is the only choice which eliminates the sentence fragment by adding a main clause.

52. **(5)** The sentence is correct. Names of astronomical bodies are capitalized. (3) is incorrect because only the name "Halley" is capitalized to show that this is *his* comet being referred to. (1) is wrong since Halley's name is not capitalized. (2) and (4) add commas which separate the subject and the verb.

53. **(3)** "Sadly" is an adverb. Since the verb in this sentence "grew" is a linking verb, it requires an adjective, not an adverb. (1) is wrong since the word "losing" is misspelled. (2) uses an incorrect form of the past tense of the verb "to grow." (4) adds a comma which confuses the meaning of the sentence.

54. **(2)** The subject of the sentence is "pies." The preposition "by" needs to be followed by an object. "Her" is an object pronoun. (1) not only uses the subject pronoun "she," but also misspells "always." The verb in (3) does not agree with the plural subject, "pies." (4) incorrectly uses a reflexive pronoun.

55. **(2)** Titles of shows and movies are expressed in quotation marks. (1) incorrectly changes the noun "fans" into a possessive. (3) and (4) not only incorrectly express "musicals" as a possessive noun, but (3) neglects to use quotation marks, while (4) incorrectly uses a colon.

Appendix: Glossary of Terms

WRITING

APPENDIX: GLOSSARY OF TERMS

Action verb—an action verb is a word located in the predicate of a sentence which tells what the subject does.

Adjective—a word that modifies a noun or pronoun; tells which one, what kind, or how many.

Adverb—modifies a verb by telling how, when, or where. Adverbs also modify adjectives and other adverbs.

Clarity—being as clear or easy to understand as possible.

Clause—a group of words containing a subject and a verb, yet not expressing a complete thought.

Cluster web—a technique used for brainstorming ideas. One idea leads to another idea, and so on. Ideas are quickly jotted down in "map" form.

Coherence—when all the paragraphs of an essay are connected to each other logically, the essay has coherence.

Collective noun—names a group of people, places, or things. Is considered as a single unit.

Colon—[:] a punctuation mark which is always preceded by a complete sentence. Used after the greeting in a business letter and precedes a list.

Comma—[,] a punctuation mark which is used to combine two or more simple sentences, interruptions within a sentence, introductory words, and items in a list. Commas also separate the day and year when writing dates, and the city and state or city and country when writing addresses.

Command (imperative)—a sentence in which an order is given.

Common noun—names a person, place, or thing in general.

Complex sentence—a sentence which contains at least one main clause and at least one dependent clause.

Compound object—when a verb has two or more objects joined by the word "and."

Compound subject—when a sentence has two or more subjects joined by the word "and."

Conjunction—a word that joins together different parts of the sentence. Most common conjunctions are "and," "but," and "or."

Dependent clause—a group of words that contains a subject and verb, but does not express a complete thought. Used in complex sentences to modify a main clause.

Direct object—follows an action verb, "receiving" its action. Can be either a noun or pronoun.

Ellipsis—[…] a punctuation mark used to indicate words are missing from a quotation.

Exclamation point—[!] a punctuation mark used to indicate excitement.

Free-writing—a technique of writing down a word and any other ideas you associate with it. A way of generating ideas.

Future tenses—indicate actions expected to occur sometime in the future.

   future simple—indicates an action expected to happen sometime in the future.

   future progressive—indicates an action that will be in progress at some future time.

   future perfect—indicates an action that will be complete prior to another action beginning.

Generalization—a sentence expressing an idea or drawing a conclusion based on facts or examples.

Helping verb—part of the verb which helps show its tense.

Homonym—words which sound the same but have different meanings and/or spellings.

Indefinite pronoun—does not refer to a definite person or thing, but rather an unspecified person or thing. Can be singular or plural.

Indirect object—noun or pronoun that tells for whom or to whom an action has been done.

Inside address—name and address of the person to whom a business letter is being sent.

Linking verb—expresses a "state of being" because it links the subject to a word which describes it.

Main clause—a group of words within a complex sentence which contains a subject and a verb. With correct punctuation, could be considered a sentence.

Misplaced modifier—when the modifier is not correctly placed as closely as possible to the word it describes.

Modifier—a word or clause which gives additional, more specific meaning to another word. Adjectives and adverbs are modifiers.

Non-countable nouns—nouns which are impossible to count, such as nouns which name emotions, or nouns which cannot be counted unless they are divided into countable units.

Object of the preposition—the noun or pronoun in a prepositional phrase.

Outline—a method of organizing ideas into a logical format. Arranges ideas into main ideas and supporting detail.

Parallel structure—agreement in sentence structure in which all the similar parts of a sentence are written in similar ways.

Past tenses—used to indicate an action that has been completed.

   past simple—used to indicate an action that has been completed.

past progressive—used to indicate an action that was in progress until it was interrupted.

past perfect—see perfect tenses.

Perfect tenses—always written with a helping verb.

present perfect—expresses an action that began in the past, but continues into the future.

past perfect—expresses an action that occurred in the past, but is mentioned now.

future perfect—expresses an action that will have been completed at a specific time in the future.

Period—[.] a punctuation mark that completes sentences.

Possession—a noun or pronoun that shows ownership.

Predicate—the part of the sentence that tells what the subject does or is. Always contains a verb and may contain some modifiers or prepositional phrases.

Predicate adjective—used with a linking verb, it links the subject to an adjective.

Predicate noun—used with a linking verb, it links the subject to a noun.

Preposition—word used with a noun or pronoun to indicate a thing's location or function.

Prepositional phrase—a preposition and its object.

Present tenses—indicate actions taking place at the present time.

present simple—expresses an action that occurs regularly on an on-going basis.

present progressive—indicates that an action is in progress right now.

present perfect—indicates an action that began in the past, but is completed in the present.

Prewriting—first stage of the writing process. Purpose of writing is established; ideas are generated and organized.

Progressive form of the verb—used to indicate an action in progress at any given time. (See past, present, future, and perfect tenses.)

Pronoun—a word used to refer to people, places, or things (nouns) that have already been mentioned, or to indefinite people, places, or things.

Proofreading—last stage of the writing process. Writing is checked over to locate errors in spelling, punctuation, or usage.

Proper noun—specific names of people, places, or things.

Question (interrogative)—a sentence that asks a question.

Question mark—[?] a punctuation mark used at the end of an interrogative sentence.

Quotation mark—[" "] a punctuation mark used to indicate the exact words used by another speaker or writer. Also used when writing the titles of TV shows, poems, short stories, and book chapters.

Reflexive pronoun—refers back to the subject of the sentence. Used to provide emphasis.

Relative pronoun—introduces clauses that act as adjectives. Can be either subject or object pronouns.

Resume—a summary of a job-seekers work experience, educational background, skills, and strengths. Must clearly state career objectives, and should provide potential employers with a brief summary of a candidate's qualifications.

Return address—address of the person writing a business letter. Includes the date the letter was written.

Rough draft—a middle stage of the writing process. Once the prewriting stage has been completed, the writer uses the prewriting planning in order to begin writing. Should consist of an introductory paragraph, paragraphs of supporting evidence, and a conclusion. All material in a rough draft is subject to revision and reorganization.

Run-on sentence—a sentence incorrectly punctuated or containing too much information. Can be corrected by making the run-on into several shorter sentences, and/or by improving the punctuation.

Salutation—the word "dear," followed by the name of the person to whom a business letter has been sent. A colon is always used after the person's name.

Semicolon—[;] a punctuation mark used to separate two main clauses that the writer wishes to have read as one sentence because they contain ideas which are somehow connected. Takes the place of either a period or a comma and a conjunction.

Sentence—a group of words that makes sense, expresses a complete thought, and ends with a period, exclamation point, or question mark.

Sentence fragment—a group of words that only expresses a segment of a complete thought.

Subject—the topic of the sentence; states what or who the sentence is about.

Subject/verb agreement—a necessity for grammatical correctness. A singular subject must be written with a singular form of the verb in the predicate of the sentence, as must a plural subject agree with a plural form of the verb.

Thesis—the main idea of an essay. The entire essay must at all times refer to or support the thesis.

Topic sentence—a sentence which contains the main point of a paragraph. The entire paragraph must be built around the topic sentence.

Transition—a smooth change from one point to the next in an essay. Transitions can be accomplished with one word, such as "secondly," or with an entire phrase, such as "on the other hand."

Voicing—a proofreading technique in which the writer reads what has been written aloud in order to hear errors that may have been missed by sight proofreading.

Writing process—the procedure followed by both amateur and professional writers. Consists of the following stages: prewriting, writing a rough draft, revision, and proofreading.